So You Wanna Be a Sexy Bitch

So You Wanna Be a Sexy Bitch

Raise Your Game from Overlooked Nice Girl to Skilled Chick Everyone Wants to Get With

FLIC EVERETT

Ulysses Press

Author acknowledgments:
Thanks to S. Buckley for his useful insights into men,
and to all my lovely female friends, who don't need this book at all.

The publishers have generously given permission to use quotations
from the works cited on page 120.

Published in the United States by
Ulysses Press
P.O. Box 3440
Berkeley, CA 94703
www.ulyssespress.com

ISBN 1-56975-451-9
Library of Congress Control Number: 2004110118

First published as *How to be a Sex Goddess* in Great Britain
in 2004 by Carlton Books Limited.

Printed in Canada by Transcontinental Printing

1 3 5 7 9 8 6 4 2

Cover artwork: gettyimages.com
Cover design: Jake Flaherty

Distributed in the U.S.A. by Publishers Group West

contents

introduction

It seems that modern life is full of instructions. Once it was considered enough simply to have your own teeth and get yourself out of bed in the morning without electric shock therapy. Nowadays, if you're not simultaneously whipping up the perfect sponge cake, negotiating a pay raise, and dropping a dress size in a week, the self-help industry regards you as a dismal failure. So reading this book is not meant to be yet another stressful challenge. This book does not state that unless you memorize all the tips within you will fail the ensuing sexy-bitch exam. Or that if you don't immediately dump your existing wardrobe, develop a breathy purr, and start sucking your finger whenever a man comes within a few feet of you, you'll never have satisfying sex. There's already enough pressure on women to be some kind of weird fantasy figure—and the last thing I want to do is add to it.

So for our purposes, learning to be a sexy bitch is simply learning to be a more confident, more self-loving version of who you already are. Most women, sadly, are riddled with doubts and insecurities, and we waste untold amounts of energy fretting about minuscule flaws and imagined defects that no one else will ever notice or care about. The benefit of becoming a sexy bitch is not that you will suddenly be able to perform a series of naked back flips into the bedroom before presenting your Britney-size butt for inspection. It's simply that you will feel sexier. Whether you're with the man you've been married to for 20 years or some guy you met at a club last night, or you're merely slumped on the sofa with your housemate, wondering whether fluoride in the water has killed all the eligible men in your town, it doesn't matter. Because if you feel sexy inside, you'll project sexy to the world, and the world will respond accordingly.

If you find some of the suggestions here embarrassing, or stupid, don't do them. If you feel spastic in stilettos, stick with flats. If you look at the pictures, and snort "Yeah, right! Like I'm really gonna do THAT after a day from hell at work," fair enough. Pour yourself a nice glass of wine and watch TV instead. The kind of sexy bitch you want to be is entirely up to you—not your man, your friends, or even the authors of books.

Ultimately, it all comes down to the old self-help truism: feeling good about yourself. And as far as I'm concerned, the one area of life where that matters most is sex. Who cares if you can't bake cakes? Who gives a hoot if you can't negotiate your way out of a paper bag or you don't know how to dress to minimize wide calves? Get a life. What matters is whether you can communicate with another person, whether you can show someone what makes you feel great and make that person them feel great in return, and have the confidence in yourself that comes from believing you're truly desirable and lovable. That's what being a sexy bitch is all about—everything else is just icing on the store-bought cake.

1 what makes a sexy bitch?

"Sex appeal is 50 percent what you've got and 50 percent what people think you've got."

—*Sophia Loren*

I think you already know what I'm going to say first: anyone can be a sexy bitch. You don't need butt-length blonde hair or hips that undulate like a belly dancer's—you can be tiny or tall, fat or thin, beautiful or, well…, facially challenged. And you can still entrance men with your sexuality. For a truly sexy woman, men will move mountains, crawl over broken glass to the ends of the earth, rescue kittens stuck up redwood trees, hang themselves upside down across the Grand Canyon, and generally make grade-A fools of themselves. All to be near you and, if they're lucky, to be in bed with you.

The most ordinary-looking women are capable of charming and disarming the most gorgeous men simply because they are sexy bitches in disguise. But their sexy-bitch status isn't conferred on them because of their looks, or clothes, or hairstyle, though all these things can help. The true difference between an attractive woman and a sexy bitch is easy to define: it's attitude.

HOW TO GET SEXY BITCH ATTITUDE

CONFIDENCE   A true sexy bitch has confidence in herself. When a man compliments her on her body, she does not reply "Oh my God! You must be joking! I'm huge!" She doesn't give men the chance to judge her and find her wanting by investing their opinions with too much power.

If a man is rude, or thoughtless, or insensitive, she walks away. She doesn't stick around hoping she'll be the one to change him. She knows exactly what she wants, and, more importantly, she understands precisely what she needs from a sexual encounter, or a relationship. And if she's unlikely to be satisfied, she doesn't pursue it. In short, she knows she's gorgeous and she deserves the best. This is not arrogance—it's pure self-belief. Basically, no one treats her badly—they wouldn't dare to.

GOOD SENSE OF HUMOR   Sexy bitches have a sense of humor. Any number of women can be beautiful: they can put on a bedroom performance like Diane Lane on speed and they can gaze adoringly into his eyes. But without the vital spark that comes from experience, native wit, and the innate understanding of other people that make up a good sense

inner and outer beauty

The bad news is that about 0.1 percent of us are natural sexy bitches. However, the up-side is that the other 99.9 percent can learn those skills and achieve sexy-bitch status without the help of plastic surgery, hair dye, liposuction, or ten hours a day at the gym. Of course, you can do all that if you really want to, but at the end of the day you may run the risk of being a very fit, very slim neurotic. No man will

of humor, the whole encounter can be as ⋯
able doll, especially one with a leak. Sexy bit⋯
ing jokes—a barrage of gags can kill any sexu⋯
However, they know exactly when to break any ⋯
phere with a little bit of humor—like when the condo⋯
for the third time.

RELAXATION So what's the final key to identifying a sexy ⋯
relaxed, so comfortable with herself that she listens properly to ⋯
and talks easily. A neurotic, hyperactive woman will never be a ⋯
bitch—she's far too concerned with what other people think of her, for⋯
ever panicking about the impression she's making and the clothes she's
wearing. She displays all the nervous body language of a purebred whip-
pet, fiddling with her hair and picking at her nails. An unrelaxed person
makes everyone else tense. In any social—or sexual—situation, a real
sexy bitch is completely chill, sensual in her touches, calm in her own skin,
and as relaxed as a cat by the fireside.

want to go to bed with you just in case you turn into a Bunny Boiler
the morning after.

Sexy bitches don't seem to be trying too hard. If you turn up at a
party with a mahogany tan, surgically honed limbs, a cloud of perox-
ide hair, and a dress the size of Barbie's hanky, for sure, some men will
want to sleep with you. But they'll also assume you're desperate for
attention and very insecure—and right after you've had sex they'll be
happy to call you a cab to whisk you out of their lives before you get
too troublesome. This is not the effect you desire, trust me.

s not to say that physical appearance counts for nothing: it

without wanting to sound like your mother (but being fully

hat I probably do), you need to realize that almost always

tch beauty comes from "Making the Most of What You've

It's not from copying Scarlett Johansson's hair, going on the

e diet as Jennifer Aniston, putting on your eyeliner the way your

st friend does, or buying insane, hillbilly clothes because a maga-

ne said they were in vogue. Fashion is not the same thing as style,

and every aspiring sexy bitch should have that simple fact tattooed

over her heart.

Sexy-bitch beauty also relies on your accepting your age. While you can certainly enhance your looks—I'm all for using wrinkle-defying creams, touching up your roots, plucking your eyebrows, and the like—actively refuting the calendar is a dangerous game to play. Dressing too young for your age is a terrible way to defy your age. All it does is highlight the vast discrepancy between teeny-weeny teenage garments and your somewhat larger limbs and boobs. When choosing clothes, any woman over 25 should ask herself, "Would the average 15-year-old wear this?" If the answer is "yes," then think very carefully indeed before buying.

Of course, it cuts both ways, and the under-45s should not be caught dead in 1980s-style piecrust collars and badly cut sensible skirts—nor should the over-45s, for that matter, if they want to continue to be sexy bitches. Be wary of fashion trends that never really worked the first time around. I'm thinking lime green, overalls, pinafore dresses. By all means, keep current and move with the times, but know yourself well enough to let your unique personality shine through and select your wardrobe according to what works for you. It's all about dressing appropriately, highlighting the good stuff and minimizing the bad.

dress to impress

Get help if you have the color sense of a drunken bat and the innate style of a Marilyn Manson. Like Bridget Jones's mother, get your "colors done" to find out whether you're better suited to brights or neutrals and edit your wardrobe accordingly. Alternatively, consider a wardrobe of separates that you know works well for you. Ask a friend to accompany you shopping and beg her (or him—gay men are the perfect honest shopping companions) to be brutally frank. It's simple, really. If you have good legs, buy a well-tailored short skirt. Lumpy knees but a great bust? Wear pants with low-cut tops. Spend as much as you can afford on well-cut clothes in natural, sensual fabrics. They hang better, feel nicer, and make you want to swish around, murmuring, "Because I'm worth it."

A sexy bitch knows it's better to have three great outfits rather than 60 different tops and skirts that are inexpensive but fall apart the first time you wash them. You wouldn't shampoo your hair with dish detergent and still expect to look good, so why wear badly made clothes and expect to feel sexy? Being poor, by the way, is no excuse. You can buy secondhand designer clothes from thrift shops or go to sample sales. There are many urban sex bitches who have nurtured a talent for never buying retail. I, however, do spend a lot on shoes. Every aspiring sexy bitch needs at least one indulgence, and Marc Jacobs footwear is mine.

your crowning glory

The next thing you need is a decent haircut. Not because it will attract men (most straight men wouldn't know John Frieda from John Malkovich), but simply because a great cut makes you feel fantastic, so you project confidence, sex appeal, and self-belief wherever you go.

Again, go to the best salon you can afford and don't be bullied into trying something "directional." Women who mumble, "Well, I don't know really, what do you think?" to some scissors-wielding megalomaniac are just asking for trouble. Take charge and show the hairstylist pictures of cuts you admire. Be persistent and demand the cut that shapes your face, falls easily into place without needing an hour of straightening irons and styling products every morning, and looks as though a man could run his fingers through it without getting them tangled up in style complexities.

The best hair color for you depends entirely on the rest of your coloring. You can dye it any shade you want, but if your skin tone doesn't match your hair, you'll look more like Edward Scissorhands than a glossy-tressed beauty. Go blonde only if you're not deathly pale and your natural hair color isn't so dark your roots become an issue every three days. Red hair doesn't suit pink complexions, but brown does. Black hair is not a good look for most women; it's deeply draining, so do it only if you've got olive skin. And "fun" colors like blue and pink work only if you've got the fashion sense to match—bright green hair and a Donna Karan suit looks more like a practical joke than a style.

making up isn't so hard to do

Then there's makeup. It goes without saying that a face resembling Cleopatra's death mask is not terribly attractive. Like men with full-grown beards, women with heavy caked-on makeup always look as if they've got something to hide. Acne, hideous scars, piggy little eyes—while you may have none of these imperfections, passersby will be suspicious because you've done such a number on yourself. Again, when it comes to makeup, the key words are "relaxation" and "confidence."

A good moisturizer is absolutely vital. Buy the best you can, otherwise your foundation will soon become patchy and you'll look like a dog that's rolled in mud. Foundation should be as pale and as close to your skin tone as possible—ask the saleswoman for help choosing your shade. Never try to give yourself a tan with it—you'll just look freakish. Your desert-island essentials are: blusher (use a tiny amount to avoid enormous 1980s stripes down your face); eyebrow pencil

> **TIP**
>
> Makeup brushes are a handy way of applying cosmetics. They give your face a glossy, professional finish and make you feel glamorously old-fashioned.

(well-shaped brows make the face—if you need proof, look at before and after photos of Julia Roberts or Elizabeth Hurley); brown or black mascara to open up your eyes and make you look interested, even when you're not; and the most essential product of all, a lipstick or tinted gloss to keep the focus on your pouty, kiss-worthy lips. You might also want to apply powder, to prevent your skin from shining too much. Other than that, forget it. Cosmetic fads like glitter, blue lipstick, and glow-in-the-dark eyeliner come and go for a reason: they don't suit anyone. Just because some stunning 16-year-old occasionally gets away with it on a catwalk doesn't mean you can too. (Which is why you can always find green mascara in the half-price basket at the drugstore.)

the body beautiful

Often it's body image that stops many a wannabe sexy bitch in her tracks. Convinced that unless she is the size of a Chihuahua she'll never be sexy, she hides herself in huge sweaters, hunches over to conceal her stomach, and generally tries to stay under the radar. So, of course, she's not alluring.

I know no one will believe me (and sometimes I have a hard time convincing myself, particularly after I've polished off the second crème brûlée), but here's the truth: Men Find All Shapes and Sizes of Women a Turn-On. Some even think sex with a skinny woman is like riding a bicycle. Others find flab frightening. Some like their women medium size, others prefer petite, while some love them tall. Basically, as Osgood says at the end of the classic movie *Some Like It Hot*, "Well, nobody's perfect." And if they are, they're probably really dull people who would rather spend a spare hour pounding away on a treadmill or climbing to nowhere on a StairMaster than drinking wine with friends, losing themselves in a great book, or having fabulous sex for hours on end.

"well, nobody's perfect"

What it comes down to is not "Am I thin/toned/shapely enough?" but "Do I accept and like who I am enough?" If the answer is no, then ask yourself why. Those who reply, "Because I'm a disgusting person who's weak and a failure" should forget the gym for now and head straight to therapy without passing Go. Others who say, "Because I've put on weight and I feel less energetic and attractive" can soon straighten themselves out by using some willpower, eating less and getting more exercise.

But a word of warning: There's nothing at all sexy about chattering on endlessly about your diet. Your friends, your colleagues, and your men won't give a flying Frappuccino what you think about Dr. Atkins or South Beach. All that matters to them is that you like and accept yourself as you are. Telling your date you've lost five pounds in a week by eating only cabbage soup will not entice him. He'll simply imagine you crouched like some madwoman over a pot of bubbling green glop, and he'll wonder why dieting is so important to you that you deprive yourself of pleasure—not to mention risk the nasty side effects.

If you are trying to lose weight, keep quiet and get on with it. I find the no-carbs-in-the-evening system works for me and avoids the pangs of complete carbohydrate withdrawal. You don't get hungry, you lose weight, and you can still drink alcohol. And if, like me, you find the gym a torture chamber of mindless pain, seek out a more enjoyable way to burn calories, whether it's dancing, gardening, swimming, having sex, or skating, and do it three times a week. Before starting any exercise routine, be sure to seek medical advice, especially if you are overweight, are taking medication, or suffer from any health problems.

If you decide life's too short for all this deprivation and exhaustion, fine. You just have to make the decision to like yourself the way you are and take a solemn vow to never, ever ask a sexual partner if he thinks you're too fat. Why torture yourself like that, unless you're a complete masochist. If he answers yes, you'll be devastated, and should he say no, you'll decide he's just being nice. So deal with it yourself.

groomed for success

As far as appearance goes, the true sexy bitch wears whatever she wants and looks just the way she wants to—but she is always groomed. By which I don't mean all prissy pearl necklaces and velvet headbands, like some society gal; I mean clean and fresh—everywhere from her hair to her teeth, her hands to her toes—and looking as though she'd be nice to touch. She's clean and sexy and smells nice. Soft skin with a sheen of body lotion is more sexy bitch-like than dry, scaly patches, buffed or varnished toenails are more appealing than yellowing claws, and shaved legs and a trim bikini line will give you more confidence than a sprawling Teutonic bush that escapes from your Lycra. You know you could strip down at a moment's notice and all would be in order. A real sexy bitch looks as though she cares about herself. If you don't love and respect yourself, why should anyone else? Present an image that's like a sack of dirty laundry and, honey, you'll get treated like one. It's sad but true: first impressions count.

> **TIP**
>
> A sexy bitch is always well groomed, which means being manicured and pedicured and having soft, smooth skin and shiny hair—all things that reflect good health and fertility.

Of course, all sexy bitches have bad days and suffer from PMS or stomach flu; all occasionally look like they got dressed in the dark or passed out on the couch with their face pressed into a textured throw pillow. But they have attitude and they knew how to work what they've got. Be inspired. So you've got all the basics: you're thinking more about attitude and you might even buy a nice pair of pants that flatter your butt. Hell, you always brush your teeth. Now it's time to learn some seriously sexy-bitch moves.

2 flirting: using your moves

"I generally avoid temptation unless I can't resist."
—*Mae West*

Anyone can flirt but the truth is that not everyone can do it effectively. We all know how to toss our hair and how to run our tongue over our lips suggestively, but unless it's carefully done you run the very real risk of looking like a drag queen, rather than a creature of mystery. Good flirting is subtle. A true sexy bitch is an excellent flirt, but she never appears desperate. There's a world of difference between body language that eases communication and opens up interesting sensual possibilities and the kind that shrieks "I haven't been laid for six months—what are you going to do about it?" As a sexy-bitch wannabe, obviously, you'll be aiming for the former.

stage one: meeting

So you're in a bar, or a gym, or an art gallery, or any of the other normal venues where male and female strangers congregate. You could even be in court, but if you're the defendant, try to save your hot moves for later. You spot someone you think would go nicely with you, but he's not looking at you. So what do you do? Avoid anything cheesy, such as sending over a drink—he'll assume you're crazy about him, and whatever transpires from this, you'll always be on the wrong foot for having initiated the chase. Ideally, you want him to think that he spotted you first. OK, it's depressing, it goes against all feminist principles, and it's a dismal throwback, but the truth is that most men like to do the chasing, at least initially. So fixate your eyes on him. It's weird but true that everyone knows when they're being stared at, and it has probably something to do with our Stone Age defense system, when the forests were full of people trying to kill the juicy mammoth first. As he turns to locate the source of the staring, flick your eyes away quickly.

Repeat the maneuver until your eyes "accidentally" meet, then look down as if a little puzzled, allowing a small smile to play on your lips. Ideally, at this point, he will come over. If not, wait a little while and then repeat your stare-and-flick routine.

And should it fail once again, you may conclude that he's just not interested and save yourself a lot of heartache. Perhaps he's just fallen in love with a supermodel who works with starving orphans and wrote her doctoral thesis on the *Kama Sutra*. You'll never know. So don't feel bad. Just pick someone else to flirt with.

stage two: talking

Let's assume that you've found your fellow and he's now standing in front of you. A true sexy bitch won't get all touchy-feely right away—that's so obvious you may as well lift up your top and ask him to sign your breasts. You want to create the impression that you're quite interested in what he has to say and you certainly don't find him unattractive, without actually making it clear that given half a chance you'd lock him away in your bedroom and never let him go.

One cunning way of doing this is to create a shared world for the two of you. A line such as "Is it just me or does everyone else in here look like the cast of *The Bold and the Beautiful*?" (or *Cocoon*, or *The Sopranos*, depending on where you are) will suggest that he is the only person like you in the whole place, which is a very intimate suggestion without actually being a statement of intent. You are also creating a feeling that the rest of the world is dropping away and there are only the two of you left.

Smile more than you normally would—not goofy, tail-wagging grins, just slow, almost-reluctant smiles that imply you didn't really intend to smile but you're having such a good time you just can't help it. You can also afford to laugh at his jokes once or twice, but make sure you have an appealing laugh. Many a man has been terrified off by a woman's donkeylike hee-hawing or her nerve-jangling shriek. A warm, low murmur of amusement is a lot better than a snorting cackle. Pretend you're on the radio and ask yourself whether your listeners would leap up to change the station, or laugh along with you.

A good flirt is never nervous; confidence is the key to successful flirting. So when he compliments you on your appearance, don't reply, "I look a mess, actually. I'm only wearing this because my girlfriend borrowed the top I really wanted to wear." Instead, say, "Thanks, you don't look so bad yourself." Gabbing inanely and offering way too much information are also the enemies of successful flirting. Hold back and offer your thoughts strictly on a need-to-know basis. Topics to avoid as you flirt include: politics, illness, depression, your ex, his ex, money, how long you've been single, and why you're a disaster with men. Don't bombard him with probing questions about his life and work—he'll feel as if he's being interviewed. A simple exchange of witty banter is all that's required at this stage.

body language

If talking is the bread, then body language is the meat in your flirtation sandwich. Actions speak louder than words, and while what you're saying can be perfectly innocuous, what you're doing as you say it makes all the difference. The main thing, of course, is lots and lots of eye contact. Hold his gaze, look down and glance up occasionally from under your lashes—but don't do it too often and make sure you never look over his shoulder, as if you're scanning for something (or someone) more interesting in the distance. If you really are attracted to him, your pupils will dilate. This has a stunning effect on men. In clinical experiments, male subjects

> **TIP**
>
> Playing with your jewelry is a surefire way of drawing attention to your charms in a certain area—like your lovely neck, for instance.

consistently pick out women with larger pupils as being more attractive because it's a sign of sexual excitement and, therefore, willingness. If you'd like your pupils to dilate and you're not sure his looks are enough on their own, just think about the last really good sex you had—even if it was by yourself. And don't look at bright lights or your pupils will shrivel so fast you'll look like a heroin addict.

While overt touching can be too much right away, you can make plenty of moves that will draw his attention to all the right areas. Most important is the angle of your body. Stand or sit facing him directly, so your attention can be focused entirely on each other. If you cross your legs, point your upper foot toward him—pointing away suggests a desire to turn your entire body away from the conversation. If they're not crossed, point your knees toward him and, if you're standing, lean in slightly. When you speak, even if the place isn't that loud, position yourself close to his ear. Shouting is not intimate, but a close, low-voiced comment is. By talking more quietly, as well, you'll encourage him to lean farther toward you, so he doesn't miss a moment of your sparkling conversation.

To draw his attention to your best features, idly trail your fingers along your necklace if you have a fine bust, or rest your hand on your knee if your legs are great. But if you've got a lovely J.Lo or Beyoncé butt, remember, you're not a baboon—you'll just have to wait for him to notice it. When it comes to your hair, forget tossing it around—you'll look like a demented Alexis Colby from *Dynasty* having a bitch fight (see drag queens, earlier). What you can do, however, is to allow a strand or two to escape—not only does this soften your face and make you look appealingly vulnerable, but it also means he can lean over and tuck it back into place. Playing with your hair, however, simply makes you look at best coy, at worst positively remedial. Leave it alone—the best flirtation body language is calm, relaxed, and open.

Crossing your arms is the body-language equivalent of "fuck off," whereas keeping your arms open and your wrists exposed is a sign of trust. Even if on the inside you're a bag of neurotic butterflies, he doesn't need to know that—and he won't, unless you tell him.

light touching

Once you're at ease with each other, and flirting has progressed from hair-smoothing and knee-pointing to the stage where you know both that you like each other, you can start to touch him, lightly and sensually, to make your intentions perfectly clear. Not all over—you're a sexy bitch, not a hooker—just light brushes with your fingertips to indicate that you really like him.

A quick touch on the knee to emphasize what you're saying is a good starting point. You

> **TIP**
>
> Take the opportunity to touch him whenever you can. A playful cuddle is always a useful way to get close—and who knows what it might lead to?

can also use the old brushing-invisible-fluff-off-the-shirt trick, but go carefully with this one or there's a significant danger that you'll remind him of his mother and he'll be afraid you're about to spit on a hanky and wipe his face clean. A simple lean-forward-and-flick motion is fine. But don't start grooming him like a female gibbon picking fleas off her mate.

Another intimate little move is to pick up his wrist and turn it so you can see the time on his watch—although avoid doing this while he's holding a drink. If you smoke, you can make use of the old film noir technique where you hold his hand to steady the flame, while looking upward into his eyes; this is pretty blatant, so should be used only when a definite attraction has already been established. Don't try the old trick of blowing a stream of smoke in his face, though—it's really not pleasant.

Good reasons for flirting

There are good and bad reasons for flirting. Sexy bitches only flirt for the right ones. These include:

1. Because you're attracted to him.
2. Because you're making yourself feel good but only when he's doing the same thing and there's no intent on either side.
3. Because you've been together for ages and flirting livens things up no end.
4. You're also allowed to flirt with close male friends, as long as they don't have overly jealous girlfriends, just to get in a bit of practice.

Bad reasons for flirting

1. To make your boyfriend jealous.
2. To try to recapture an ex who dumped you because you hope it might lead to sex that will make you feel loved, albeit briefly.
3. To annoy girls you don't like by flirting with their boyfriends or husbands right in front of them.

Beware: nine times out of ten, bad-reason flirting will backfire on you. The ex will sleep with you and you'll wake up redumped and humiliated, or you'll gain a nasty reputation for being a cock tease and a woman who can't be trusted. Your boyfriend will go and sleep with someone else in retaliation, or you'll have a huge fight. So when you are about to start flirting, first stop and ask yourself what your intentions are. If in doubt, stop batting those eyelashes at once.

Forget corny and creaky maneuvers such as "palm reading"—it's as transparent as a polished aquarium. Also avoid the weary "I seem to have something in my eye," *Brief Encounter* gambit, although, admittedly, it worked a little too well for Celia Johnson.

You can make your intentions perfectly clear by touching his forearm or the soft skin above his elbow as you talk (ideally performed as if you're barely aware of what you're doing, simply implying that you're physically drawn to him on some subconscious level). Or lightly squeeze his hand during a moment of particular emphasis in the conversation. Of course, as all these small touches and subtle maneuvers go on, he will almost certainly be flirting back at you—the only difference is that, as a sexy bitch, you'll be doing it better.

anti-flirting

A sexy bitch almost never finds herself in a situation she'd rather avoid, because she has the tactics to extricate herself before it all goes wrong. Many untrained sexy bitches, however, make the mistake of being too encouraging to men who should by rights be squatting on lily pads, secreting poison. Not because they want to lure these creepy individuals on, but simply because they don't know how to get rid of them. Luckily, there are ways of repelling men without causing them to become offensive. It's just a matter of creating a shield around yourself that they cannot pass, try as they might.

Anti-flirting begins with no eye contact. As you refuse that drink, avoid looking into his eyes. Everyone knows the eyes are the pathway to the soul and offer instant access to all your feelings of guilt, embarrassment, and the desire to make everyone like you. Truth is,

TOP TEN FLIRTING TRICKS

1. Maintain eye contact but make sure you smile at the same time, or else you'll look like a crazy stalker.
2. Look down then up at him, as if sneaking a quick glance—very sexy.
3. Raise your eyebrows and smile when you're impressed with what he's telling you.
4. Don't reveal too much about yourself—let him ask first.
5. Lean in to speak directly into his ear.
6. Sway to the music—most people assume that sensual dancers are great in bed.
7. Don't bitch about other women or you'll look petty and insecure.
8. Accept compliments easily—never argue that he's wrong about what he thinks of you.
9. Brush your fingertips lightly across his arm or knee during conversation.
10. Keep it light—make jokes, not serious points about the world.

you have no need to feel guilty—you didn't ask him to approach you and you owe him nothing. The whole encounter is his responsibility; all you need to do is get rid of him. A sexy bitch knows that not everyone has to like her—the only people whose opinions matter are the ones she likes.

If you are positioned near him, angle your body away from him. If you feel you must talk to him, make your answers brief. And if he has the nerve to make physical contact with you, slide out immediately from his touch—never give him the impression that he is permitted access to your body. Forget the classic victim's excuse, "I didn't want to offend him." Ask a nearby employee of whatever place you're in to remove him, or get a sympathetic male to help you out—and if there is really is no one suitable around, invent a jealous boyfriend and predict his imminent return. You know all about not accepting drinks you haven't seen poured, not leaving a stranger in charge of your wine while you go to the bathroom, and all that, don't you?

Of course, you may know the creepy guy. Maybe he works in your office, he's working on your house, or he lives next door—in which case you'll need to spell it out. You could also ask a male relative or friend to tell him to leave you alone. Be careful not to send mixed signals. You may be agreeing to a drink because he seems lonely, but he's reading your gesture as "I want you, Tiger." So watch it. Sexy bitch or not, no sensible woman would ever put herself in the path of danger if she could reasonably avoid it.

longterm flirting

Of course, in any serious relationship you're not always going to be flirting over breakfast like Bogie and Bacall:

- "You know how to whistle, don't you?"
- "What? Why are you always asking me stupid questions when I'm trying to read the paper?"

Naturally, there are obstacles to the sort of flirtatious exchange you enjoyed when you first met, and that is an entirely normal part of an evolving relationship. You can, however, discover ways to "sex it up" between you with a subtlety and humor you both will enjoy. To reinject flirting with your longtime love, though, you're going to have to make a bit of an effort. However sexy bitch-like you are, it's probably not going to happen in your home, surrounded by kids or bills, or with the TV blaring and the washing machine clunking. You need to go out on a date again and remind him that you actually are a sexy bitch—you simply got sidetracked from your true purpose by domesticity. Here's your chance to rekindle those lovely moments of your early infatuation.

Choose a nicely lit hotel bar or restaurant and do not, under any circumstances, be tempted to meet up with friends at any stage of the evening. That's really not the point. Dress up, arrive separately, and make a pact beforehand that you will not talk about the kids, or work, or how much your home improvements are going to cost.

You have to make time to be romantic.

It's not going to happen by accident. You don't have to spend a fortune to have a romantic evening. And you don't need to go to a fancy restaurant. You can have just as great an experience shopping for a luxurious dinner for two and cooking it together, or packing a picnic and whisking yourselves off to a park or a riverbank. Stay in, turn up the furnace, dress up, and have a picnic in the living room. It's also nice to share the stuff that interests you. The aim is to remind yourselves of what attracted you to each other at first, before real life crept in, so keep the conversation light, sprinkled with wit and charm, and intersperse your nuggets of banter with plenty of hand stroking and gazing into each other's eyes. If you feel this is all somewhat contrived, take the pressure off by just going to the movies. But while you're there, if you don't want to snuggle up together in public, at least hold hands. You know how to hold hands, don't you? You just put your palms together and squeeze.

3 seduction and foreplay

"I'll come and make love to you at five o'clock. If I'm late, start without me."
—*Tallulah Bankhead*

It can be difficult for anyone—even a sexy bitch—to know when to transform heavy flirtation into actual seduction. It's often an awkward moment, when noses bump or zippers get stuck. As a trainee sexy bitch, you need to know how to move seamlessly from gazing into each other's eyes to slowly exploring each other's mouths, and then beyond. There comes a point, however, when it's easier to continue your lovemaking than to back off, clear your throat, and offer to make a cup of coffee. So if you decide you're going to go for it, it's helpful to pinpoint this Seduction Moment.

You can, of course, wait for him to make the lip-locking first move. Sometimes there's just one look or moment between you and all else falls into place quite naturally. However, if he seems unsure about whether you're really interested in him, you need to make it clear. A friend of mine simply leans forward and kisses the guy in mid-sentence—an effective but brave maneuver. If that kind of action's too drastic for you, wait for him to pause for breath and then let your eyes deliberately drop to his mouth. You may even reach out and idly trail your hand down his arm, or stroke his fingers or even his face. If he fails to get the message after this, he may well be brain-dead, in which case, what are you doing seducing him?

If you're prepared to give him one last chance, maintain your gaze on his lips while leaning very slightly forward—exactly the way it happens in movies when a couple is about to kiss and at the last minute something dramatic prevents them. Ideally, in your case nothing will, and you'll melt together painlessly. If he's shy, you'll need to do all of the above, but slower. If you are both shy, you will have to decide

TIP

The neck is packed with nerve endings and a light trail of kisses here can drive a man wild.

whether you would rather miss a golden opportunity than risk embarrassment. The truth is, it's not hard to tell if someone's interested. If he makes all the right moves but pulls back at the last minute, he's a champion game player and you're better off without him.

kissing with confidence

You might think everyone can kiss. But you'd be wrong. An alarming number of people assume that all they have to do is press their lips together and rotate their tongues for a bit. This is not, however, how a sexy bitch kisses, and rightly so. A real kiss—the kind that makes him catch his breath to prevent being overcome by erotic feelings and collapsing at your feet—requires a lot more than that. The basic tech-

KISSING TIPS

Kissing isn't as easy as it looks. There's an art to it, and clamping your mouths together and hoping for the best isn't it. A great kiss can be as good as sex, and sometimes better, because it's filled with promise as well as eroticism. So if you've never been quite sure you were doing it right, follow the advice below and you can't go wrong. And if his kiss isn't working for you, you might be able to improve it.

1. Let your lips brush together a couple of times before you home in. This builds tension and arouses all the nerve endings in your lips.

2. Always make sure your breath is extra-fresh. It sounds obvious, but after a night of drinking and smoking, it's so going to smell like a bar-room floor. So eat a mint first, at least.

3. If he really can't kiss, the best way to retrain him is to simply say, "Can I just tell you a little kissing trick that drives me wild with desire? Just keep still and I'll show you." Then proceed to kiss him exactly as you want to be kissed. It can't fail—all men want to drive women wild with desire.

4. Break off during the kiss to reposition your lips. This stimulates different nerves and makes sure the erotic charge keeps being released. There's nothing duller than a kiss where nobody moves.

5. Use your hands, too. Caress the back of his neck or run your fingers through his hair. Passionate clutching of his back is also a good move, as is sliding your hand inside his shirt or T-shirt, depending how far you want the kiss to go, of course.

nique is to begin with a gentle pressure on the lips and gradually part them. A few more delicate presses on the sides of his mouth, then brush your lips up and down over his, by now also parted, lips. There are thousands of nerve endings in the lips, and your aim should be to stimulate every one of them.

All this comes before any tongue action. When you do introduce it, be subtle: no one wants their mouth forcefully invaded. Allow the tip of your tongue to dart out to meet his, and, as your passion builds, you can gradually entwine your tongue with his. Move it gently in an exploratory fashion—never let it lie in his mouth like a damp rag. Don't leave your tongue inside for too long though; keep breaking away and returning to lip kissing in order to build up the anticipation.

Sometimes you can move away from his mouth altogether and kiss his neck, just below his ear. For many people, this is a major erogenous zone. Combine the kissing with a little stroking of his hair, neck, or face, or with body caressing and…bang, you're off and running. If you're going to bite the neck area, though, be gentle. Most men won't appreciate a giant purple bruise blooming above their collars. Once you've mastered the art of sexy bitch kissing, you can move on to explore the rest of him.

how to touch him

So long as you're not too heavy-handed or completely out of sync with each other, most sensory touching feels quite nice, but there's a world of difference between "quite nice," and "Oh, my God." Clearly, as a sexy bitch you'll be aiming for the latter. Grasping a handful of

EROTIC MASSAGE

Experiment with touching by practicing some massage strokes on your man, and hopefully he'll return the favor. The following instructions aren't exactly a massage, more of a prolonged exercise in the Art of Tease, and he will appreciate it as such.

1. Begin at his neck. Lightly stroke the base where it joins his collarbone and, at the same time, gently squeeze the back of his neck to make him feel instantly relaxed, yet extremely turned on. The neck is a very vulnerable area of the body, and by caressing him here you're creating a deeply intimate connection that's based on trust. Once you've gained his trust, you can do anything, right?

2. Now run your fingers down his spine or slide your palms along it, rocking your hand slightly, to stimulate both sides of his back. Once you reach the base, lightly scratch your nails down his buttocks, before kneading them firmly.

3. Trail your hands along his inner and outer thighs and stroke the tops and soles of his feet with a firm sweep of your hand (otherwise it just feels ticklish and he'll probably either inadvertently kick you or giggle).

4. Now turn him over and touch his front; areas to concentrate on first include his hips, particularly the hollows just beneath them, and his stomach. It doesn't matter whether he has a washboard or a pillow, all stomachs respond well to gentle circling of the fingers, especially when you allow them to drift down toward his groin and teasingly pull back. Many men love to have their frequently neglected sides caressed too, with light, sweeping motions up toward the chest.

the back of his sweater while wondering how you're going to get his jeans undone is not the best a man can get, believe me.

Sensual touch is a combination of tease and pressure. You want him to anticipate that you're heading for his erogenous zones, without actually touching them yet, while at the same time stimulating all his nerve endings so he's driven crazy with desire. A word about nipples. For most men, nipple touching is as personal as their taste in underwear, and, without asking, it's almost impossible to guess what he wants. While some men adore a nipple squeeze, a light pinch, or a gently circling fingertip, others shudder in horror at the very idea. The only way to find out is to ask. You don't have to bring a halt to proceedings—a simple, murmured, "Does that feel nice?" will suffice.

> **TIP**
>
> A gentle massage is a sensual way to touch each other, but remember to involve each other's genitals at an early stage—otherwise it's all too easy to fall asleep halfway through.

Arm stroking is a bit girly for many men, unlike most women, who love to be caressed all over with a fluttering touch. Men prefer any touching action to have a purpose. Basically, if they believe you're making them feel good shortly before heading straight down to their penis, they're happy. On the other hand, if they think you're engaged on some nebulous tactile journey, they're likely to get bored and will attempt to push your hand downward after a few minutes. While you're stroking and caressing him, keep reminding him of the ultimate goal: sweep one hand close to his genitals, even brush across them— and then prolong the teasing. That way, he'll be excited, not frustrated.

getting the right touch from him

Obviously, when it comes to touch, he can't possibly complain about your technique. However, when it comes to being touched, your challenge is to persuade him to do what you want without nagging or criticizing him, or making him think he's an inept ham-handed fool. In the anxiety to please a new partner, some men may be a little awkward, so give him the benefit of the doubt at first.

A lot of men are unsure when it comes to touching a woman. They've spent so long engaged in pleasing themselves (look, I'm sorry but it's true) that they naturally assume you want to be touched in the same way—firm, direct, and straight to the genitals. Of course, women are more like artichokes. To please you, he must nibble his way through lots of layers, which are enjoyable to toy with in their own right, before he gets right to the heart—your clitoris. There are two ways of teaching him this. The first and most traditional one is simply to guide his hands, to wriggle away in a coquettish manner every time he makes a beeline for your genitals, and to make all the right noises when he does the right things but stay quiet when things are less than exciting. Now this may work if he's the one man alive who understands exquisite subtlety, grew up with five sisters, has learned to decode the sighs and groans of women at 20 paces, and also has a Ph.D. in psychology. However, if he's a regular guy who didn't do these things, all you will end up with is him wondering why you're huffing and puffing and won't let him stroke you for two minutes without writhing around like a harpooned sand-shark. So you might find that the second, less traditional, teaching method works better. Read on...

Be up-front

Tell him what you want. It's that easy. Like many women, you may now be clasping your hands like a coy Southern belle, murmuring, "Oh, I couldn't. It's embarrassing. He'll think I'm demanding, he'll think he doesn't satisfy me...." Admittedly, it's hard to start laying down guidelines on the first night, though even then a simple "Mmm, that feels amazing, just a little to the right" shouldn't offend anyone. But if you intend to be with this man for more than 12 hours, do you really want to set up a pattern where he does it all wrong for you and you act like it's fine, a routine that could go on forever? Of course, a stream of barked instructions—"OK, OK, touch me there. Harder. No, now. Rub me. Yes. No. You've slowed down, speed up"— will make him feel more like a NASA mechanic than your lover and he may well send you spiralling into space accordingly. But there are subtler ways to tell him how to turn you on and any man worth making love to will be grateful for the information. A simple "That feels wonderful—could you do it even a tiny bit faster?" is fine as long as you sound happy rather than irritable. Or "I don't really come during sex, but if you could rub me afterward that would be fantastic." And if you're really lucky, "Oh God. Please, hard as you can. You feel incredible."

Use lots of positive adjectives and excitable tones. Compliment him and encourage him. Think of your man as a dog who's eager to please, but doesn't know if you want him to bring you the paper or your slippers. He needs kindly direction and lots of praise. It's better to do this in bed (or wherever you make love) than over dinner. Otherwise, you run the risk of its being more like an analyst's session: "You know when you do that weird thing with your lips? What's going on there?" isn't nearly as sexy as "Oh, yes, don't stop" in the throes of passion.

Consider that what works for one woman may not do the same for another. He may have been in a longterm relationship and got used to pleasing one partner. You will need to make him feel at ease and appreciated, while gently leading him in the right direction.

his favorite thing

It is not exactly that it's all about his penis or anything—without it, he'd probably be just as happy going fishing or watching sports on TV. Because for a man, a whole lot of sex really does come down to what his penis is feeling, which is why they're all so obsessed by size and judge their manliness accordingly. Therefore, it pays for you, a sexy bitch in the making, to know exactly how to handle your man's penis. You'd think it would be easy, right? But you'd be amazed just how many women don't know how to manage a simple erection. For a start, some penises can look a bit purple and even threatening or perhaps a little off-putting. But if you think of his penis as his vulnerable alter ego, your attitude will be transformed. You will want to do right by him and, as we all know, you have to give a little to get a little.

You can add all sorts of fancy strokes to your basic hand job. The "two hander," where you massage the base at the same time as the tip, is always enjoyable. Try the "shaft massage," which is exactly what it says. Flex your fingers all the way up and back down. Or you can simply tease him by running your fingers around the head, while

HANDLE WITH CARE

Most men prefer a firm grip on their penis. Unfortunately, many women make the fundamental error—just as some men can do with women—of handling a penis in the same way they'd enjoy having their clitoris fondled: gently and delicately. But his favorite thing is far more robust than that. He needs to be held confidently or you won't get the necessary rhythm going, and the friction will be lackluster, to say the least.

1. So grasp his penis in your right (or left) hand as if you're holding onto a glass and don't want it to slip—obviously you're not squeezing so hard it will break, either. Your little finger should be at the base and your thumb round the top. That leaves your other hand free for fondling balls, nipples, anus, thighs, and so on, as desired.

2. Once you've got the grip right (don't worry, he'll let you know—he's had years of practice), you can begin to move your hand up and down. The skin of his penis should move but your fingers shouldn't shift at all—the action is all in the wrist.

3. If he's circumcised or has a tight foreskin that won't move back and forth easily, you may need to move your fingers. Lubrication—a pea-size amount, as it says on the tube—should do the job.

4. Then build up your speed gradually until you're rubbing as fast as you can without hurting your wrist. However, always keep the rhythm steady—no sudden pulls or jerks, and no grinding to a halt just as he's beginning to gasp.

stroking the frenulum—the tiny bit of skin joining the head and shaft—with your thumb.

Once you've got the basic method down, the rest should come easily, as it were. When he starts to come, the most sexy-bitch thing you can do is to lean down and swallow his semen. If that's about as appealing as eating a bucket of slugs (really, it's not that bad, but some women are terribly fastidious), the second best thing is to allow him to come all over your breasts. This is always a good one combined with the penis-rubbing-between-the-breasts technique. Failing that, let him ejaculate on your butt or, if he's after a dirty porn–type experience, your face. But if you're not feeling that generous, there's always your stomach. What, still a no? Then point his penis toward his stomach. The bonus to this option is that the sheets won't get messed up. Have some tissues handy by the bed, too—there's nothing quite so odd as the feeling of sperm drying on the skin.

And when it comes to his touching your clitoris the right way, make sure he returns the compliment. Tell him exactly what you want him to do—he'll love it, and so will you.

Oral sex

Possibly one of the greatest inventions known to man, and woman, is oral sex. It can, however, be fraught with difficulty because women are so often nervous about receiving it and wary of giving it. We worry about how we look, taste, and smell. We fret that he might be bored and when it comes to giving blowjobs, we're too often torn between the fear of getting it wrong and the pain of a numb jaw.

There are ways to make oral sex nothing but enjoyable—and they're very simple.

how to receive it

Having him go down on you is a lovely display of trust and passion. If he's down there, it's because he wants to be, so don't ruin it by muttering, "Oh no, God, I haven't taken a shower for at least an hour." If you're that worried, take one just before you come to bed and rest assured that men are programmed to find the smell and taste of a healthy vagina perfectly erotic. If he isn't doing what you like with his tongue, there is a relatively foolproof method that virtually guarantees oral orgasm, which you can teach him. To begin, he should part your labia gently with his thumb and forefinger then locate your clitoris with his tongue. But instead of licking all over it randomly, he should simply flick his tongue back and forth across the "hood" of the clitoris and around the edges, where sensitivity is at its height. If he also pushes a finger slowly in and out of your vagina at the same time, you should soon be coming 'round the mountain, in no uncertain terms.

> **TIP**
>
> If you like what he's doing, gently hold his head exactly where it is. And if you don't, tell him what you want instead. Because "I want" really does get you somewhere when it comes to oral sex.

Remember that if he's bothering to do this, it's because he wants to please you— so show him exactly what you want and don't just lie there wishing he'd get it over with as he frantically nibbles the wrong spot. Sometimes men are too rough, allow their teeth to nip you, or

TOP FIVE FOREPLAY TIPS

1. A massage may sound a bit dull, but for the stressed out sexy bitch, it's an invaluable way to get in the mood for sex. Explain to him that if he devotes 20 minutes to kneading and stroking you, you'll devote 20 minutes to licking and sucking him and you should have a bargain.

2. If you're struggling to get yourself in the mood, focus on a very sexual memory and recall how you felt and what you could hear, see, smell, and taste. This way, you can reconnect with how it felt to be deeply sexually involved, and your brain will trigger the same chemicals and endorphins.

3. Don't ignore the area called the perineum—between his balls and bottom. It responds remarkably well to light pressure, or small circles of your fingertip. Don't press too hard, but if you combine it with a hand job, he'll be your slave forever. Probably.

4. Teach him to kiss your neck and ears as well as your breasts. Many men go straight for the obvious body parts, but most women have deeply erogenous zones around the sides of the neck and just below the ears. Light kissing or licking around these areas can be almost as good as an orgasm and certainly makes you want one pretty fast.

5. Most women need to be seduced relatively slowly. So if he makes a habit of grabbing your nipples and expecting instant delight, remind him that, generally, kissing comes first. It brings you closer emotionally, it's deeply intimate, and you'll be much more inclined to get your nipples out afterward. If you can't remember the last time you had good sex, there's something very wrong, but it can easily be sorted out.

even imagine that violent sucking is a good idea. In which case, tell him it isn't. His next girlfriend will thank you for it.

how to give it

Giving a blowjob is not always a simple case of "you just put your lips together and suck." While that will keep him happy for quite some time, there are more sophisticated techniques that will ensure you're both enjoying yourselves.

One of the most important considerations is your position. Lying down with your head between his legs will last about two minutes, until it starts to hurt. The best ways to give a comfortable blowjob are: one, lying at right angles to his body, with your head sideways on his lap; and two, kneeling between his legs while he sits upright. The first way works because you can angle his penis to bump against your cheek, not your tonsils, which removes all risk of gagging. If it still feels too big, flex your jaw and he'll pop farther out whether he wants to or not.

> **TIP**
>
> Make sure you are in a comfortable position; otherwise you'll get a crick in your neck and an aching jaw before he's finished.

You can supplement your mouth with your hand around the base and rub in rhythm with your head movements. Start off reasonably slowly, with your lips closed around the head of his penis, just taking the shaft into your mouth and out a little way. As he gets more excited you can speed up. By using your hand, you can save yourself the exhaustion of bobbing your head frantically. Because your mouth's a bit freer this way, you can also use your tongue to stroke and caress the tip or to flick along the shaft.

You can supplement the basic blowjob technique with a mouthful of warm liquid, or champagne, which feels incredible swirled around his sensitive parts. But make sure you keep your lips clamped shut, and your teeth firmly out of the way. You can also pay his balls attention—licking, sucking, and gentle fondling will all feel marvellous, but nibbling, pulling, and squeezing will not. You can try 69, which involves your simultaneously going down on each other, but it can be difficult to focus on what you're feeling and what you're doing at the same time: it is a good party trick if you can manage it.

The big question, of course, is "spit or swallow?" It's entirely up to you, but swallowing is very generous and very sexy. Just let it all hit the back of your throat, hold it in your mouth, and keep your tongue still if you don't want to taste it. Then gulp. And you can always have a drink straight afterward. If you spit, be discreet—it's only kind, after all.

4 the dirty sexy bitch

"There are no good girls gone wrong, just bad girls found out."

—Mae West

Listen carefully, aspiring sexy bitches. There's a world of difference between "dirty sexy bitch" and "dirty slut." Dirty sluts have no self-respect and will let a man do whatever he wants, however degrading. Dirty sexy bitches, however, enjoy the raunch potential of sex.

They know that good sex isn't all about candlelight, soft music, and gentle caresses. Sometimes only hard, filthy fucking will do. But that kind of sex doesn't mean your partner won't respect you, or that you have to degrade yourself. So long as you want to do it, and you're equally turned on, you can be as dirty as you like without any worries. And if you're not happy with something, you tell him so. You don't say, "OK, I'll do it with all your friends from the bar so you'll like me more." Because dirty sexy bitch sex is only as dirty as you want it to be.

what to wear to bed

It's easier to tell you what not to wear first. Avoid anything featuring cartoon characters, cute slogans like "Cuddle Me" or "I Need a Hug" or anything made of brushed cotton. Unless he has a granny fetish, it's unlikely he'll be tempted to find out what's underneath your floral-sprigged, tent-size nightie. Boudoir wear is an art. If you're planning to be a sexy bitch, it's not acceptable to throw on a ripped, old oversize T-shirt every night. Comfortable though it is, it's not a look that screams "Take me." Your partner may feel that you are taking him for granted and failing to make an effort. Of course, lots of women—and men—like to sleep naked. There's no harm in that and it certainly encourages bodily contact, but it's a little like serving the dessert before you've had the appetizer—it kind of ruins the surprise. Men's sexuality is based largely on anticipation, so for him, it's far more exciting to present yourself as a delightful present ready to be slowly unwrapped rather than as a wholesome Swedish type who's about to go hiking *au naturel*.

> **TIP**
>
> Sexy underwear doesn't have to be uncomfortable—in fact, the easier it is to wear, the sexier you'll feel in it.

Most likely, he will make the final decision on what he wants to wear in bed, and, sadly, the options for sexy male bedroom wear are limited. A fresh pair of underpants to show off his shape will probably work for you. If you're choosing a seduction outfit for him, bear in mind that cotton, silk, or nothing at all suits all men and, as with your own bedroom wear, avoid any with cartoons or slogans. I hardly need to mention that posing pouches are about as sexy as paunches, do I? Thought not.

Despite the great variety of gorgeous lingerie shops, some men are still really bad at buying sex wear for women. Crotchless scarlet lace rarely enhances anybody's labia, unless theirs happens to be particularly stunning. If he's buying for you, head him in the direction of one of the many lingerie emporiums offering edgy, sexy, but well-made items. Rather than nylon nasties you'll be getting something that will feel great against your skin and put you in the mood. Convince him that this is something that will ultimately benefit him.

And as for sleeping, there are plenty of sexy nightgowns that won't compromise comfort or style—train your eyes to slide past anything featuring cartoon sheep. Although sex wear is not the same thing as sleepwear, the two can be combined in the form of, say, a see-through baby-doll. However, do set aside your selection of boudoir wear for special romantic occasions; there'll be no doubt as to what's on the agenda if he sees you in this. Your sex wear should consist of at least one outfit (or single item) that enhances all your assets and makes you feel devastatingly sexy.

When buying underwear, don't worry about whether the items will show under clothes. Instead, ask yourself, "Do I look like a million dollars in this?" Look for lace (though not the scarlet scratchy kind), silk, satin, ribbons, mesh, and bows. Cleavage-enhancing corsetry or tight-fitting but silky gowns will show off your figure. Most men are wildly excited by red or purple underwear, so consider deviating from basic black. Obviously, avoid stretch nylon, sporty cotton, and anything serviceable that looks as though you could carry shopping home in it. Pretty G-strings are great, small panties fine, but big, sensible butt grippers are not. The best ones are those that tie at the sides—like a strippers

Admittedly, some men like virginal white underwear. But if you're unsure, go for the "classy whore" look—it'll get you everywhere. Make sure your bras are professionally fitted—four breasts are not a good look. Hate your stomach? Buy a vintage-style, wide, lacy garter belt to give you an air of 1950s glamor, or choose a bustier or a corset, to which you can attach stockings.

Ah yes, hosiery....There are some men who actually prefer pantyhose, but they tend to have grown up in the 1970s, when "American tan" was not yet a term of abuse. On the whole, you're safer with stockings. Go for black, barely black, or fishnet. Unless you are very thin or getting married, avoid white hosiery—they'll make your legs look like undercooked sausages.

For guaranteed sex appeal, you are much safer with stockings or lace hold-ups. At the very sight of stockings, he'll be guaranteed to cheer with excitement. They look great, provide easy access to underwear (which always goes on top of garters, never underneath), and they tap directly into every man's sexual fantasies. Generally, garters are sexier than hold-ups because they are more traditional and they don't leave strange pink elastic marks around your thighs. If they're just too fiddly to put on, leave the hold-ups on throughout sex and he'll be so excited, he'll never know the difference.

accessories and foot fetishes

Naturally, most women wouldn't normally wear shoes to bed. But even if you're a sporty-sneaker woman who walks like a newborn giraffe in high heels, a pair of boudoir shoes is a good investment. "Lay-me-down-and-fuck-me" shoes (as they are technically known) feature stiletto heels, ankle straps or ribbons, and pointy toes. They have the effect of elongating your legs and enhancing the curve of your butt—and also putting your man in mind of a little light bondage. Obviously, feminism is not making its presence felt here, but you can always lecture him on equal rights later, once you've tied him to the bedpost.

Of course, the old hooker standby of thigh-high boots is also a winner in the bedroom—but only if you've got legs like Julia Roberts in *Pretty Woman*, otherwise you run the risk of looking like Puss-in-Boots. Much safer are fluffy marabou mules, as worn by Marilyn Monroe and a variety of 1950s glamor models. Supplement your boudoir wear with a selection of negligées, silk wraps, peignoirs and kimonos to float around the house in. Add chiffon shawls, long strings of pearls, even chain belts, and diamond piercings—fake ones if you don't fancy suffering unnecessary pain just to draw attention to your erogenous zones.

the art of undressing

Of course, everyone knows how to undress, but not everyone can undress like a sexy bitch. When it comes to sex, just pulling off your clothes and throwing them in a heap won't do, unless you both want just a quickie. There are two types of sexy-bitch style undressing: Sexy Disrobing and Actual Stripping.

sexy disrobing

The natural moment for a little sexy disrobing is when you're getting ready for bed or changing clothes. Even if you aren't backed by a thumping audio track or don't have the energy to slink around in front of him wearing a feather boa for ten minutes, you can still offer him a treat.

Avoid taking your shoes off first—you'll immediately look much shorter and, therefore, less sexy. However this rule does not apply if you're wearing sneakers or hiking boots, so get 'em off. Remember, always leave the best until last, so next slowly remove your jeans or skirt, giving him a great view of your legs as you undo your top.

There's no harm in turning away and bending down as you do this, though you must keep your legs straight or it's no use at all as an erotic pose. Once you're down to your bra and panties, you can offer him the chance to undo your bra for you, or just whip it off. Now bend down (straight legs, remember) and slowly ease down your panties. Even skimpy G-strings or tricky garter belts can be removed elegantly if you keep your legs straight, and once your underwear is off you could even fling the item at him playfully. Straighten up and turn to face him, delightfully naked.

> **TIP**
>
> "Nineteen...twenty...coming, ready or not!" Boudoir undressing builds anticipation and makes you feel beautiful, whether you are wearing just a string of pearls or a full, matching set of underwear.

You may like to remove your shoes at this point. If you're wearing pantyhose, discount the shoe advice and remove these first—otherwise you'll look like an extra in a Jane Fonda workout video. Besides, pantyhose make it almost impossible for him to touch you or to gain access to your body, and they definitely look better under clothes than they do on their own. This method of stripping off is the simplest way to get undressed and still keep his rapt attention.

the full strip

This is a more complex but ultimately satisfying method of disrobing. Of course you'll need music to do this, otherwise you'll just resemble

TOP TEN STEPS TO SUCCESSFUL STRIPPING

1. Place your hands on the fastening of your top and stroke your fingers over the zipper or buttons to give the impression that you might just possibly be thinking about undoing them.

2. Maintaining seductive eye contact, slide the zipper down or undo the buttons, and then turn away from him and remove your top. Keeping your hands over your breasts, turn back to face him.

3. Slide your hands down to your skirt or pants fastening. Again, play with the zipper—slide it down a little one way, then back up again to tease him.

4. Undo your skirt or pants and turn away again. Now bend forward a little (straight legs, naturally) and allow your clothes to fall to the floor. If it's a small garment, kick it aside or use the toe of your shoe to toss it upward, catch it and fling it to him.

5. With your hands over your breasts, face him again and dance slowly, gliding your hands up and down your body. Slide a bra strap down and then back up to tease him. Let both straps drop but keep your bra in place with your hands. Reach behind you and unclip it, but don't let it drop yet…

6. Now turn away again so he can admire your butt. Let your bra fall, and then reach down gracefully and throw it to him while still facing away from him. Place your hands over your breasts and turn back to face him. To reveal your breasts, slowly slide your hands down to the sides

a character in some weird art-house film. Your audience (I'm assuming it's just one, but don't let me stop you) should be seated at a safe distance away from you, so there will be no touching. The whole point of the striptease is to build sexual tension, so make sure you of your panties. (You did remember to put your panties on OVER the garter suspenders, didn't you?)

7. Tease him a bit more. Pull the sides of your panties down a little way, or pretend to undo the ribbons. Push the front down as far as it will go without revealing any pubic hair. Turn around again and slip your panties down, then step out of them neatly. Kick them aside, or to him.

8. Nearly there. Except for shoes and stockings, you are now naked and it's perfectly acceptable to stop at this point if you want. But if you prefer full nudity, take off your shoes. Standing on one leg, undo each buckle. (If you're less flexible, place one foot at a time on the bed, or rest your foot on the chair he's sitting on and slowly roll each stocking down, then pull it off with a flick of the wrist.) Reach down to unclip your garter belt and whip it away.

9. Continue to dance in front of him just out of reach until he can't bear it another second. You may then cross the room and begin to undress him.

10. If you're shy (and most of us are when it comes to taking off our clothes in a lit room), conceal as you reveal with a strategically placed feather boa. You can also add glamorous old-school accessories such as elbow-length gloves, a string of beads or a silk scarf. Use them to add to your performance, covering yourself with the boa or scarf as you slowly remove your lingerie.

move close to him as you dance and then writhe away frustratingly at the last minute. Your audio track should have a good, thumping, dirty beat—R&B goes down well—and make sure it's slow enough for you to remove your clothes in a leisurely fashion. Try to avoid flinging everything off randomly in a desperate bid to keep up with the music. The whole experience should be relaxed and sensuous for you both.

Wear clothes that are easy to remove, such as slippery satin. Avoid fiddly buttons, pants in general, and anything you have to squeeze over your head—hurricane hair is not a sexy look. A dress that does up at the front is ideal, or a front-fastening top and a split skirt. Underneath, wear stockings or hold-ups, panties, a bra or a bustier and, of course, the ubiquitous high heels so beloved of all men. Once you are dressed, the music is ready, and you have some props on hand, you can follow the Top Ten Steps to Successful Stripping on pages 46–47.

male stripping

While there may be some women out there who get immensely turned on at the idea of watching a man strip, I don't know many of them. Women are less visually aroused than men at the sight of a naked body of the opposite sex, possibly because, unless they're having sex or taking a shower, naked men tend to look slightly ridiculous, even a little vulnerable. But if it floats your boat to watch him prancing around to "Rock Your Body" in white socks and a G-string, go girl. If not, then come join the rest of us and take his clothes off for him.

> **TIP**
>
> A word of advice to men: G-strings are a bad idea. He may be looking great in his jeans, but catch a glimpse of the posing pouch beneath them and it's an instant lust-killer.

Start by slowly unbuttoning his shirt, then slide it off. Run your fingers around to his belt buckle, and undo it. Unzip his trousers, put your hands on his hips, and push, so his jeans and underwear come off together. This only works if he's not wearing shoes; so if he is, help him to take them off first.

talking dirty

To be a true sexy bitch you need to cover all the senses. Looking good and smelling sweet—even having silken skin that tastes of rose petals—is not enough on its own. You've got to talk it like you walk it; in other words, you need to learn to talk dirty. Of course you can have silent passionate sex, the only sound being the rustle of sheets and maybe the creak of knee joints. It can be quite exciting to stifle your orgasm at times; for example when you're staying with family or having sex somewhere you shouldn't. But sometimes you need to voice your thoughts out loud if you want your true desires to be fulfilled—and most men are as responsive to this as a cat is to the sound of a can opener.

Sexy bitch or not, the trouble is that dirty talk doesn't come naturally to most of us. For a start, "dirty" words are generally the ones we've been taught as nice little girls never, ever to use. Overcoming the vision of your mother gasping in horror and disgust can be tough enough, and then there's the question of how to make your string of smut sound raunchy and convincing enough and not like an 11-year-old trying to impress her girlfriends.

Rather than waiting until you're mid-sex, and then blurting out, "Fuck me harder with your...er, um, your...well, OK, your rod," it pays to have a vague plan regarding the kind of things you can say that will turn both of you on. On the whole, men are aroused by earthy sexual language and like you to be direct. It won't do you any good if you ramble on about his putting his jade stalk into your scarlet love box—he may well assume you've begun collecting Chinese artifacts and wonder why you're bringing it up just now, mid-thrust.

Most men like plain, straightforward words, words that do what they say on the label, such as "cum," "fuck," and "cunt." If just reading this is making you cringe, you may need a little practice. Some women find the word "cunt" offensive, though they are quite happy using male-oriented sex slang. Of course, what you say needs to turn you on as well, so if talking like a fourth-century warlord on a pillaging spree fails to drive you crazy with desire, a compromise should be reached.

building your sex lexicon

If you're a shy sexy bitch, the best way to begin to talk dirty is to establish the kind of things you'd like to say to your partner. Sit down with your man and the both of you write down 20 words or phrases that turn you on. For inspiration, look at published erotica, think of scenes from your favorite movies, or simply rummage through the dark closets of your sexual psyches. When you've finished, take turns reading out loud a phrase each—yours might be "I love your beautiful body," while his could be the more direct: "I want to fill you with my hot cum." Either way, you'll soon find out what excites your partner. Then swap and read each other's list out loud. Vary your speed and tone, put on a French or Italian accent, and have fun. The idea is to get used to speaking the words out loud. He may have no problem saying the word "fuck," but really struggle with "love." You might find "gorgeous" really easy, but clam up over "cock." It's like learning a foreign language, so practice until you both feel comfortable and you can start putting words together.

talking in bed together

So you've learned to talk dirty while fully clothed and sitting at the kitchen table, giggling like schoolkids. The hard part (see how easily it slips out?) is to do this in the throes of passion. Begin during foreplay so you get used to the sound of each other's voices. Describe how you're feeling—a simple "God, that's fantastic!" will suffice. As the action heats up, so will your words, and hopefully, before you know it, you'll be giving each other an erotic running commentary. Bear in mind, though, that unless it's used sparingly, talking dirty can soon turn into a tedious monologue. You don't want to be begging for his hot tool only to find he's gone to look for his earplugs.

the sexy bitch and porn

Porn can be a fraught subject. Most women don't enjoy the thought of their partners flicking through a magazine full of 17-year-olds with breasts bigger than their IQs, or the idea of him masturbating over some on-screen stunner. It can make us feel insecure and jealous and that's not to mention any stronger feelings we may harbor about the role of porn and its often-misogynist image. If you hate porn, fair enough—I won't suggest you get over it and learn to love the sight of eight jiggling boobs and one squashed-looking guy, who's supposed to encapsulate all our fantasies. While most porn is still aimed at men, the good news is that sections of the industry are finally waking up to

TOP PORN TIPS FOR DIRTY SEXY BITCHES

1. *Nerve* magazine (www.nerve.com) provides a wealth of couple-friendly erotica: stories, confessionals, and a library of erotic photos from the early days of photography ("Hold this fern and look winsome, Alicia") to more recent styles ("Cup your boob job, Shannon"). Either way, it works.

2. Cliterati (www.cliterati.co.uk) is a site where women post their own sexual fantasies. Some are appallingly written, others merely dull, while still more…well, it's nice to know others are having the same thoughts. The site is helpfully divided into Straight, Gay, Taboo, and so on.

3. Nancy Friday, perhaps the pioneer of sexual openness, has produced a series of fantastic books of women's (and one of men's) sexual fantasies. *My Secret Garden*, *Forbidden Flowers*, *Women on Top*, and *Men in Love* are jam-packed with things you may never have considered fantasizing about before, but now that you mention it….

4. Join an organization or go to events that promote women's sexuality: Cake (www.cakenyc.com) is dedicated to promoting women's sexuality in a positive light (more fun than it sounds) and regularly hosts huge parties with male and female lap dancers, party-goers in skimpy costumes, and exotic dancers. No men are allowed in without a woman, so it's a safe, fun place to drop your inhibitions.

5. The Lover's Guide, a popular video series, features real couples making love in an entertaining and instructive fashion. It's mainly entertaining, though, and it's porn for people who object to the fakeness of most erotic filmmaking. This is the real thing, with the loving aspect included. It's stylishly lit, decently scripted, and very female-friendly.

the notion that women might want to watch something that turns them on, too. Ex-porn actress Candida Royale has produced a series of female-friendly videos and others are following. With the advent of internet retailers, there's no need to schlep around to several sex shops to choose a film. Watching porn together works well for some couples, though plenty of women find they'd rather not, due to potential insecurity. There's also the danger they may forget about sex completely and end up shrieking with laughter, saying, "What is that hair about?" or "Is that 1985 or what?" If you do want to go for it, allow your own action to develop alongside whatever's going on on-screen. Sitting side by side, watching in silence, is a little too much like frequenting a sleazy sex cinema—unless of course that idea turns you on. And if "blue movie" action doesn't work, you could always try viewing internet sites or looking at magazines together.

all in the mind

If none of the above appeals, then try women's porn (aka erotic literature). About ten years ago, publishing houses realized that many women enjoy reading about sex more than watching it. Hence the sudden flood of erotica with blurry black-and-white photos of orgasmic women on the front covers, breathlessly titled *The Blue Pearl* or *The Taming of Theresa*, and so on. The stories generally focus on heroines who somehow keep stumbling upon cruel, hard masters and their wayward bisexual mistresses, but hey, it's more fun than reading cookbooks in bed. If the florid writing style leaves you cold, try more mainstream literature with an erotic bent, by writers such as Anaïs Nin, Colette, the Marquis de Sade (why are they all French, I wonder?), Nancy Friday, Vladimir Nabokov, or Henry Miller, or classics such as *Moll Flanders*, *Lady Chatterley's Lover*, or *Fanny Hill*. Read them out loud to each other or steal away somewhere and get yourself all worked up alone. (If you decide to read them in the bath, don't drop the book in your excitement—they're hell to dry out.)

5   xxx sex and how to have it

> "I think people should be free to engage in any sexual practices they choose; they should draw the line at goats, though."
>
> —*Elton John*

If you read magazines regularly (or even, like me, write for them regularly), you'd be forgiven for thinking that actual sex is the easiest thing in the world to get right. Your Best Sex Ever!, Make Mine a Large One—Multiple Orgasms!, Keep On Coming!: all these headlines are guaranteed to depress and trouble almost anybody. Because we're not all having this mythical great sex, we naturally assume there's something wrong with us—or else we're doing it wrong. Well, that may be true, but the genuine sexy bitch knows that intercourse is not the be-all and end-all, and that great sex, as we've discussed already, is as much about attitude as it is about action.

That said, intercourse is still pretty important and there are various ways to make it work better for both parties. If you're not in the mood, your bodies don't fit together perfectly, or you expect a multiple orgasm after three thrusts, you probably will not have Your Best

Sex Ever. So the number-one tip for all sexy bitches is Have Realistic Expectations.

great expectations

When you are having sex for the first time, both of you are going to be nervous—unless you're hopelessly drunk, in which case the chances are you won't be having great sex anyway. So expecting all that hanging-from-the-ceiling, screaming-with-joy stuff is almost certainly going to leave you disappointed with the just-average performance you'll both turn in.

But good sex isn't about any preconceived notions gleaned from glossy magazines or great cinematic moments. It's about—repeat after me—confidence and communication. Both build up over time, so first-night sex, particularly if you care about him, isn't going to be as good as third-month sex, when you can discuss what you want with ease. And if you're not emotionally involved, it can still be fantastic. As Woody Allen once said, "Sex without love is an empty experience—but as empty experiences go, it's one of the best." Don't beat yourself up over sex. If it's not perfect, read on, and you'll have all the technical knowledge at your fingertips. What only you can work out, however, is whether or not the guy's worth having sex with. So, even if you follow all the advice in the world, if the sex is still no good, the problem might be your choice of a partner.

Anyone who's ever flicked through the *Kama Sutra* will know that there are at least 200 positions for sex. Anyone who's ever learned to drive a car, however, will know that it's complicated enough to get the gears and the clutch working in harmony. Like driving, sex works best when it's smooth and simple. Don't expect to memorize hundreds of positions. It's enough to establish a repertoire of about ten, that work every time and deliver satisfaction all the way around. The following are ten of the best:

the missionary

This position is still the most popular, so it can't be bad. Missionary may be a little dull, but lying flat on your back, with him on top, gives you plenty of opportunities to kiss, knead his bottom, and thrust your hips. You can liven it up by grinding them in circles, or press your thighs together instead of opening your legs so he feels as though he's penetrating a double-length vagina. You're clenching his penis between your thighs even when he pulls out to thrust back into you. This also increases friction for you, so it's an all around winner.

girl on top

Favored by women who like to be in control, this position works particularly well if he's got a large penis because you get to control the speed and depth of his thrusting. Insecurity is the enemy of girl on top ("Do my breasts look droopy?" "Is he looking at my stomach?"). In fact, facing him from above, with your back arched so your breasts are thrust toward him, is one of the most flattering positions you can get into. It also means you can lean forward so that your clitoris grinds against his pelvic bone, and the chances of an orgasm during sex are vastly enhanced. As a bonus, he doesn't have to use his hands to support his body so he is free to touch you.

squat position

A variation of girl on top, the squat isn't dignified, but it is orgasmic. Again, you're on top, but instead of sitting down, you squat over him. Yes, it's a little like the position you'd adopt for peeing at a rock festival, but the rewards are infinitely greater. Wear high heels because your thighs will ache less. Gradually lower yourself onto his penis and lever yourself up and down by pressing your hands against his chest. This position stimulates your entire vagina, including your G-spot (if, indeed, you have one), and allows him to touch your clitoris and breasts, so it's probably the best of all positions for any sexy bitch—just as long as you have strong thighs.

off the bed

Remember Jessica Lange and Jack Nicholson in *The Postman Always Rings Twice*? Well, even if you don't, the sexual position they made famous is an Oscar winner. She was on her back (on a flour-covered kitchen table as it happens, but it's just as good on a bed) and he stood between her legs. This means your man can achieve a powerful level of thrusting, either by holding onto the bed/table, or by gripping your hips. You can also raise your legs and balance your ankles on his shoulders to allow him maximum access to your vagina, and thus increase the friction. This is a passionate, male-dominant pose, plus it's one that works well half-clothed. So it's perfect if you're in a rush, like Jessica and Jack.

standing up

Standing-up sex is much maligned because most people don't understand the basic principle. They think you have to be the same height, or that she has to fasten her legs around his waist like some tentacular giant squid. But the only standing-up sex that really works—unless he's enormous and she's tiny, in which case the giant squid thing occasionally succeeds—is when you face the wall and push against it for support and he stands behind you. Place your palms on the flat surface to give yourself some leverage and arch your back so your bottom's sticking out toward him. He can then angle himself into you and hold onto your waist, or similarly, place his hands against the wall too. This way, he can use his penis or his hands to rub your clitoris and he can also reach around to your breasts. Plus, most satisfyingly, nobody falls over. If you have a mirror alongside you, it works even better.

doggy style

Every man's favorite position, the doggy offers total stimulation, a marvellous view of your bottom, and fantasy potential for both of you because you're not gazing directly into each other's eyes. You can either kneel on all fours with your back arched and your bottom pointing invitingly upward, or leave your bottom thrust skyward while your head and shoulders lie comfortably on a pillow. Another variant is standing up and bracing your arms on a bed or table. (Be careful when balancing on the edge of the bed—one false move and it's all over.) In all options, the basic key is that he's behind you and you're offering your bottom as a major beacon of sexual delight. It's a passionate, dirty position and every sexy bitch keeps it in her repertoire for those times when you just don't feel like whispering sweet nothings (what do you mean, every time?).

BONING-UP TECHNIQUES

Here are three common problems on the erection front and ways to circumvent them.

1. If premature ejaculation is nerves-based only (and if not, consult a doctor), you can train him out of this. You need the tried and true stop-start technique, which means he enters you for one stroke, pulls out, waits for the excitement to subside, and then goes back in, like Jacques Cousteau after attaching a new oxygen tank. He stays in for a couple of strokes, exits before orgasm overtakes him, and repeats as necessary. You do need patience, but if he's stimulating you with his fingers in between, it shouldn't be too bad—quite enjoyable, in fact. You can also try the nurses' favorite technique: make a ring of your thumb and forefinger and squeeze gently but firmly just underneath the head of his penis before he's about to come.

2. If he can't get an erection at all, try a slow, gentle blowjob. And if that doesn't work, you can buy little devices called cock-rings, which fasten around the base of his penis and work to delay ejaculation while maintaining an erection. However, if it's a regular problem, he needs a medical professional to cast an eye over the situation.

3. If he can get an erection but can't orgasm, it's likely to be nerves. He should be able to relax in time as your relationship builds. Meanwhile, lay off the sex and see if he can come via a blowjob or hand job. If so, it's probably only a matter of time before his sexual nerves wear off. If not, again, he needs to consult a psychosexual therapist, which is not as scary as it sounds, to discover the emotional root of the problem.

the cat

From dog to cat…coming soon: the otter. Just kidding. The cat position has nothing to do with fur or whiskers, unless you're willing to combine it with some role-play—and please, don't let me stop you. It is, in fact, the quick way of saying coital alignment technique, which sounds like a medical procedure but is really a simple method of livening up your sex life. To do this, you lie on your back, and then he lies on top, puts his penis inside you, and inches upward until his pelvis is level with your clitoris and he's very deeply inside you. At this point, he grinds in slow circles, placing delightful pressure on your clitoris. If you want to raise the excitement level more, clench and unclench your vagina with your internal pelvic-floor muscles (as if you wanted to stop a pee mid-flow) to bring him his own catlike state of bliss.

face to face

Intimate and often impassioned, the face-to-face position is the best one for lovers who are deeply comfortable with each other. There are several variations—he sits on a chair, you straddle his lap; he kneels on the bed or floor and you kneel over him. If you're feeling particularly Tantric, he can sit cross-legged with you on his lap and you can cross your legs behind his back. You might be tempted to make faces or burst out laughing in this position, so you might feel more comfortable sticking with the less exotic poses, or keeping your eyes closed. The benefits are that you can kiss, gaze into each other's eyes, and establish a deep, emotional connection. Because the position is definitely about "making love," there's nowhere to hide; the upside is that intimacy is intensified and the sex tends to be slower and more meaningful. Not a good one to pick for a one-night stand, then.

spoons

This is the ideal sex position for lazy couples—and we're all lazy couples sometimes say, on a Sunday morning or just before dropping off to sleep on a Tuesday night. Being lazy doesn't mean you're not a sexy bitch, just that you're not prepared to work all that hard to have a good time, and that's OK. "Spoons" is so-named because your bodies fit together like spoons in a silverware drawer, facing the same way. He lies behind you (obviously, if you lie behind him, it's never going to work) and you part your legs far enough to allow his penis to enter. It helps if you bend forward a little, so that your bottom is shoved right up against him. Then he puts his arm around you, idly kisses your neck and plays with your breasts, and you rock gently, to orgasm or to sleep—whichever happens first.

facing away

Occasionally known as the reverse cowgirl—because you, the sexy bitch, straddle him, but instead of facing his head you look at his feet. Not attractive, but hopefully the physical sensations make up for the view. You must be very careful not to bend his penis backward, so when you lower yourself onto him, guide him in with your hand, then rock gently backward and forward—no thrusting up and down. You get the dazzling clitoral stimulation of his pelvic bone against you, he gets a superb view of your bottom and waist, and you can also reach under and stroke his balls. He can reach up and touch your breasts or grasp your waist, which is guaranteed to look tiny in this position.

his orgasm

For a man, having an orgasm ought to be as simple as putting a letter in a mail slot—he shoots, he scores, and he's done. But regardless of how much of a sexy bitch you are, he may have problems. In fact, sometimes it's because you're such a sexy bitch that he may not be able to cope with his own vast sexual desire for you, which can mean impotence, premature ejaculation, or just sheer, god-awful performance anxiety. The commonest expression of male performance anxiety is being really, really bad at sex. So he'll mount you and thrust violently into you like a drone impregnating the queen bee seconds before he dies. Or he'll give three little jabs of his penis and come before you've noticed he's in. Else he'll fail to get an erection and try to stuff it in anyway and hope you won't notice—you will, of course. There's only one way to deal with any and all of these symptoms and that's kindly and briskly. Gasping "Oh my God, what's happened, is it me?" will help no one. Whereas a smile and a cuddle, perhaps with a brief comment, such as, "I'm tired too. Let's do it later when we're not so exhausted," will put the incident firmly in its place without destroying his fragile self-esteem.

Of course, if he thinks he's giving you a fantastic time, you can refer to pages 31–33, which explains how to improve his sexual behavior while allowing him to think he did it all by himself. If the problem is a recurring one, there are certain techniques that can be used.

mismatched orgasm syndrome

There's one problem that's enormously common—and as a sexy bitch, it's almost certain that you'll be troubled by it at some point:

mismatched orgasm syndrome (MOS). I made up the "syndrome" bit, but it might as well be a medical fact. You may have noticed, in your sexual adventures, that men tend to come first. In fact, unless you have a clitoris mounted on the outside of your body, which leads to enormously erotic feelings every time it's brushed against, you may have realized that they *always* come first— because you haven't got a penis

and they have. The reasons why men orgasm more easily are far too complex to go into here, but basically if we don't come, we simply feel a bit fed up—whereas if they don't come, the human race grinds to a halt. So obviously, nature cares more about their orgasms.

Luckily, today's caring, sharing men like to make a woman come. We like coming. Yet to get his-and-hers-orgasms to coincide is like docking a space station blindfolded. Unless you mutually masturbate, whereby you can slow down and he can speed up, having a simultaneous orgasm is unlikely.

For most women, orgasming through intercourse means their clitoris must be consistently stimulated. For him to come, however, he needs to make jabbing, thrusting movements, which increase friction on the shaft of his penis—so it's all about the vagina. Which means—guess what—that your paths to orgasm are totally different.

The easiest way to resolve this is for him to make you come first. Either with his hand, with his tongue, by rubbing the tip of his penis against your clitoris, or with a vibrator. Then, straight after, or even during, your orgasm, he can enter you and focus on his own excite-ment. Otherwise, he'll come first and fall asleep. It's a chemical thing—he can barely fight it. And you will be left, quite literally, high and dry. So it pays to concentrate on maximizing your orgasm.

making the most of your orgasm

As you will know, if you've ever masturbated (yes, you have, I saw you), it's easy to come when you know what you're doing and nobody's watching you. It's much harder, however, when somebody else is second-guessing what you want and you're worrying about whether they're getting bored, or wondering if you're making funny noises and if your stomach looks fat.

Inhibition is the enemy of orgasm, because to come you need to be fully relaxed, physically and mentally, and you aren't going to relax when your mind is playing a loop-tape entitled "My Enormous Butt."

If you're not used to orgasming alone, I suggest you practice a lot more—come on, it's no hardship—to discover what fantasies and touches really work for you. When you're with a new partner, don't put pressure on yourself to come quickly. It takes time for anyone to find out what turns you on, and while you can help and guide him, you may find your own nerves or uncertainty are preventing your orgasm. In this case, take the pressure off both of you by explaining to him that although you're having a great time, it just isn't going to happen tonight.

all-over stroking

If you've been with your partner for a while, but you just can't shut up the internal voice that's droning on about why it's taking so long, and whether he really wants you as much as his ex, you need to learn how to overcome your inner monologue, and all-over stroking is one of the best ways to do this.

Light, feathery stroking is scientifically proven to access all the brain chemicals associated with nurturing, safety, and comfort. When you're being stroked, it's hard not to relax. So a ten-minute period of caressing before he even gets near your clitoris will almost certainly speed up your eventual orgasm. It also helps if he's focused on you and doesn't look for a second as though he could be bored. So, sucking and licking your nipples while he touches you helps, as does kissing you rather than staring into space, appearing to fantasize about Pamela Anderson and how much quicker than you she'd be. If he's getting the speed or the pressure wrong, show him what you want; don't just lie there wincing silently. Never feel guilty about fantasizing—the vast majority of women can't come without it. Besides, what he doesn't know won't hurt him. Finally, it's not unusual to take up to an hour to reach orgasm. Anything less and you're doing okay.

multiplying your orgasm

Does multiple orgasm exist? It depends on your definition of "multiple." Scientifically, it's generally assumed to mean "more than one orgasm during a sexual encounter." In which case, of course it does. If your view of multiple orgasm, however, is based on porn movies, it means "a wild, shuddering, over-acted orgasm that lasts for about three minutes and begins the moment a guy touches her." In which case, get real, what do you think? It is possible, though, to have bigger, better orgasms without going into the ins and outs of Tantric sex, which promises orgasmic greatness. (We could, but we haven't got three years to study the ways of the

Taoist masters, and you'd be so exhausted afterward you would want a vacation, not a multiple orgasm.) The simplest techniques to multi-orgasmic sex are the build-up and the return.

the build-up

This does exactly what it says on the can. He strokes and rubs you closer and closer to the point of orgasm, and then breaks off just as your breathing quickens and you think you can't bear for him to stop. By the fourth or fifth time, you will be so worked up that you'll either crack him over the head with your heaviest vibrator out of sheer frustration or you'll tip over into the biggest orgasm you've ever had.

the return

This will guarantee greatness after you've had your first orgasm. Once you've calmed down, but the genital area is still sensitive, he should get down there and lick as gently and tenderly as he can. He must not touch your clitoris—it's too sensitive. But he can flick his tongue over the area all around it. After a while, that orgasmic sensation will rebuild and when you do come, it will dwarf your previous orgasm like a tsunami crashing over a village pond. Honest.

TOP FIVE WAYS TO ORGASM

There are many kinds of orgasms and many ways to have them. So feel free to think of more than these five:

1. VIBRATOR   Possibly the easiest and quickest method of all. Switch it to the highest level, lie back, and enjoy your filthiest fantasy. It'll all be over in five minutes, unless you want it to last, of course. You can use vibrators on your breasts and nipples, too. And while some women like to insert them, others prefer to rub the tip across their clitoris.

2. ORAL SEX   As long as he uses his tongue effectively and can touch your breasts at the same time, this should be a powerful and satisfying orgasm. If you can't come through oral sex, you may be nervous about what he's thinking. It's 99.9 percent certain he's having a great time, so stop worrying.

3. MANUALLY   Correct use of his fingers on your clitoris, particularly when coupled with a finger sliding in and out of your vagina, should ensure an orgasm, but unless he knows your body well, it can take a while.

4. PENIS   If he grasps his penis and rubs the tip lightly over your clitoris, it should result in giddily orgasmic sensations for both of you. But he must not cheat and put it in. It also helps to use a little bit of lube, to make it a smoother experience for both of you.

5. G-SPOT   If his fingers are long enough, he can insert one or two into your vagina and curl the tips over your pelvic bone on the front wall. Somewhere around here should be the G-spot, a spongy area the size of a small coin. If he can stroke it, it could result in a highly impressive orgasm.

faking it

Sometimes the bitter truth is that even a sexy bitch can't come. Whatever he does, however your vibrator wriggles and jiggles and tickles inside you, however many visions of Brad Pitt, oiled and ready for action, you conjure up, the internal workings are dead. You're tired, you're feeling angry, you can't switch your mind off tomorrow's work—whatever it is, it's just not happening. But the poor guy's trying so hard, wouldn't it be easier to keep him happy and pretend?

Well, not in my opinion. If faking makes you feel better, fine, keep practicing your "Oh...Oh! God! Yes!" noises and hope they work. But I think you're not so much being kind as dishonest. Because if you behave like you're having a great time when you're not, it can become a bit of a habit. Before you know it, there's a big fault line in your relationship: you're resentful, he's confused, and all because you can't tell him how you're really feeling. It may be flattering to his ego to believe you're multiorgasmic at the flick of a switch, but it's a lot better for your relationship to be honest and admit that while it's not his fault (unless it is), you just aren't going to come right now.

If it's a one-night stand or a casual relationship, though, does it matter? Well, yes. Because, really, why on earth would you give him the satisfaction of thinking he's doing it right when he so clearly isn't? You're a sexy bitch, girl, not a groupie.

6

the single
sexy bitch

"What do I wear in bed? Why Chanel No. 5 of course."

—*Marilyn Monroe*

Being a sexy bitch isn't restricted to those occasions when you have a man around. What, so you thought you could just do your wiggly Marilyn thing every time he showed up and spend the rest of the time being a slob? I don't think so, lady. Being a sexy bitch is a full-time job, and, arguably, it's even more important when you're not seeing anybody. Self-esteem, confidence, gorgeousness—they don't just disappear like vampires at dawn the minute you become single. They need work, whatever your circumstances, if you want to maintain them throughout your life. And it's vital that you remain a sexual being even when the only man you see from one day to the next is your 85-year-old window cleaner (although admittedly, you may not want to demonstrate your skills to him). To stay a sexy bitch, you need to know how to make yourself feel sexy, even when there's no one watching.

your sexy self

As we all know by now, feeling sexy comes down to self-esteem. But it's difficult to keep reminding yourself what a hot catch you are when you haven't seen yourself naked for six months and your pubic hair has been allowed to grow more Bornean rain forest than Brazilian beach. So the first thing to do is to take a good look in the mirror. I know, I understand, the very idea of seeing The Stomach under harsh, unforgiving bathroom lights, or twisting around to view The Butt in its full, baggy glory, may not be quite the instant turn-on you're hoping for. In which case, you need to sit down first and make a list—mental or otherwise—of all the nice things your lovers have ever said about your body. If they never have (what were you doing with them in the first place?), then list the parts of your body yourself are most proud of.

mirror, mirror

With the list in mind, turn the lights right down, as low as you like (if you're really insecure, a low-wattage bulb glowing feebly from another room is perfectly acceptable), and strip down to your best underwear or full nudity, whichever you prefer, in front of a full-length mirror. Make sure you've got make-up on and your hair's brushed—we're aiming to see what a new lover would view, not a vision of what humankind might look like after a meteor hits earth—and remember your mother's advice about posture. Try to relax; you can face the reality check. Shoulders back, stomach in. You will also find that rather than standing square on, if you balance your weight slightly on one hip and turn three-quarters to the mirror, you'll look instantly thinner. For a master class in this, see Elizabeth Hurley in any photograph taken throughout her entire career.

Now, obviously, there's going to be stuff here you don't like, however you stand. You're a woman and it's in your job description not to like everything about the way you look. However, your challenge is to focus on at least six things about your face and body that you're fond of, and ignore the rest. When men look at sexy bitches, they don't think, "Hmm, great bust, but really, her ankles are a little chunky." They simply home in instantly on the bits that are best presented—and besides, even if your ankles look like redwood trunks, that's what boots are for.

touching yourself

The whole purpose of this exercise is to see yourself as an appreciative man would see you, not as a critical diet doctor. And once you've located the good parts, you need to wake them up by the power of touch. You can do this in front of the mirror or lie down for a more comfortable exploration (you may want to lie down, just in case you run the risk of falling over). It's a simple matter of caressing yourself in a way that feels sensual. So, if you do hate your tummy, ignore it. Focus on your lovely ankles or your swanlike neck and stroke yourself there instead.

Admittedly, you may feel a bit of a fool writhing around, fondling your own kneecaps, but you need to learn to accept yourself as a sensual being. If you don't do this, then every time you leave your home, you will be projecting the word, "Don't come on to me, I'm repulsive" in giant letters above your head. Strangely enough, men will pick up on that and steer clear of you. Training yourself to accept and enjoy your own body will change the attitude you project to "Whoooh, check this out, baby," or words to that effect. So there is method in the madness, believe me.

Once you've had a good feel of all your most impressive parts—and there's no hurry, you can play with your breasts for as long as you like, men would, if they had them—it's time to move on to what certain coy people like to call "self-pleasure." Mastery of masturbation can do wonders for your sexy bitch status. It makes you feel great, it gives you that glowing, sexy look that you usually get only from fantastic first-night sex, and it boosts your confidence faster than a Viagra-Prozac cocktail. And all from a flick of the wrist.

masturbation

Obviously, it doesn't make you go blind. In fact, masturbation has all sorts of benefits, such as boosting your immune system (and better than nettle tea, too), enhancing your sense of well-being, and making you more likely to win the lottery. Okay, I made that last one up, but it's still pretty good. Most women masturbate but don't talk about it. Just because the subject is as carefully concealed as our clitoris, doesn't mean it's shameful.

So throw out all those bad-girl feelings of dirtiness, shame, embarrassment, and wickedness. Or pay a good therapist to help you with this. If your mother told you God would strike you down for your exploratory childhood fiddling, I have one question: "Are you still here?" And if anyone told you that "self-abuse" was evil, ask

HOW TO SELF-AMUSE

Self-abuse is a completely old-fashioned—not to mention repressed—euphemism for masturbation. Self-amusing is a much more accurate description, particularly for a sexy bitch. So to keep your sex drive well oiled, even in fallow times. Masturbate whenever you feel the urge. Well, not when you're on the bus. I mean in private. Though there's no harm in sneaking to the bathroom at work for a quickie, as long as you can do it silently. If you're not sure how, it's really very simple.

1. Find somewhere private—if you have housemates, put the chain on the door, and if you have parents or, even worse, children who may burst in, buy a deadbolt lock for your bedroom door. That's how much you don't want to be caught masturbating, and not because it's wrong—just because it's private.

2. Now take your underpants off—you'll never get anywhere with a bunch of fabric cutting off your route to victory. Find a hand mirror and make sure the room is well-lit.

yourself, "Has an orgasm ever started a war?" Okay, Helen of Troy, but that wasn't masturbation, so it doesn't count. Forget your guilt and welcome woman's best friend: your clitoris. Get to know it, because it's time you had some fun.

Occasionally, women insist that they "don't know" if they've had an orgasm; if you have, you'll know. Because while your clitoris will stand any amount of frenzied rubbing before you come, afterward it just wants to curl up in a ball and be left alone, and that's not to mention the waves of excitement and the release of tension. So, actually, you probably do know. The more you masturbate, the more

3. Use your fingers to part your labia and have a good look. If you've never become familiar with this part of your anatomy, the little lentil-shaped thing at the top is your clitoris, the tiny hole in the middle is your urethra and the big hole at the base is, obviously, your vagina. If you're not turned on, just stroke gently around your vagina until it gets slightly wet, and then use your lubricated fingertip to circle your clitoris. If you still find the skin dragging, lubricating jelly will ease things.

4. Try out different pressures and movements until you feel strange and undeniable stirrings of excitement, then just keep going. Some women like to touch their nipples (well, one nipple) at the same time, while others enjoy pushing a vibrator or another finger in and out of their vagina. Some like to lie on a pillow and gyrate their hips against it; others will only use a vibrator on their clitoris. Basically, the end result—orgasm—is the same. You may find you come a great deal faster via masturbation than you do with a man.

you'll come to understand what works for you and the sexier you'll feel. And when you do have a partner, you'll be in a better position to explain what you want in bed.

being bi-curious

In recent years, increasing numbers of apparently straight women have been expressing their bisexual curiosity. We can assume it was always there, though it's more acceptable to explore your Sapphic side today—what with female celebrities kissing each other every time they need column inches, gay and lesbian singers crossing to the mainstream, magazines such as *Diva* "for the lesbian in you" and every other film, TV soap, and drama series featuring a lesbian or bisexual character.

There are even websites devoted to bi-curious girls, such as bi-bi-baby.com, which allows you to chat with other women like you. All of which is a complex way of saying that if other women turn you on, or you simply fantasize about having sex with them, that doesn't mean you're a lesbian and you have to undergo a major lifestyle change and come out to your parents and your boss, waving rainbow flags. It just means you're comfortable with your sexuality, and there's a hell of a lot of pretty women out there.

If you'd like to turn your curiosity into action, you can go about this in two ways—get drunk with an open-minded female friend and see how she reacts when you kiss her—or the easy way. The first is certainly an option, but as with threesomes, orgies, and the like, recruiting close friends into sexual exploration is an emotional mine-field. What if she hates it? What if you're too embarrassed to cope afterward? What if she loves it and falls for you, when you were just interested in checking out how her breasts felt? So, the second option may be safer, which is to locate a women-only or "lesbian and bi-curi-ous" club night in your local area, and go there for a chat and a dance. If that's way too scary for you, locate a lesbian-run social group for the confused and bi-curious, on the internet or in person, and make your approach. It might turn out that, when faced with the reality, you're not as keen as you thought you were or it may be the begin-ning of a whole new lifestyle. Just don't tell men, or you'll be doomed to a lifetime of "Can I watch?" requests.

the sensual world

Just feeling sexy isn't enough for a true sexy bitch. Your whole world should be appealingly sensual. Floating about in silks and satins and masturbating more often than a 15-year-old boy on a *Playboy* shoot will not work if your living environment is a mound of discarded take-out cartons, old newspapers, and dirty underwear. To live as a sexy bitch, your surroundings must be sexed-up, too. If your living space looks more like a dentist's waiting room (harsh overhead lights, furniture pushed against walls) than a Turkish opium den, it needs fixing. When you open your door, you want to feel that your place expresses who you are, whether that's sporty and sexy, or girly and sexy, or any other permutation of sexy you care to name.

Colors that enhance the sensuality of a room include reds, pinks, oranges, browns, and

> **TIP**
>
> Using textures such as fur and velvet can turn your room from a drab box into sensual retreat—you may never even want to leave home again. Silks, satins, furs, and velvets can make a bed so desirable that you'll just have to invite someone to join you there.

golds. Try black, but use it sparingly with pink or red. White is relaxing and an all-white room can offer a feeling of deep calm and peace, which can be highly sensual. But if you overdo it, it can look like an operating room. Liven up your walls with colorful framed pictures or prints—original art is more personal and dynamic than the same print two million others bought. It doesn't have to cost anything—most of us are capable of making something attractive to hang on the wall,

TOP TEN WAYS TO SEX UP YOUR SINGLE LIFE

You may be going nowhere but to bed alone, but that's no reason not to make an effort.

1. VIBRATOR   Every woman's "other" best friend. You need a vibrator to provide quick, easy orgasms at the flick of a switch. Try the small seven-inch three-speed type. It's subtle and relatively stylish and does the job.

2. PERFUME   Always smell nice. It doesn't matter if you're not going anywhere. A spray of scent on your pulse points and hair will clothe you in a sensual waft of fragrance all day long. Try lots of brands before you decide which is your signature scent.

3. UNDERWEAR   Even if the only time anyone's going to see your underwear is if you're taken to the hospital after an accident, you should still make sure it's nice. It doesn't have to match exactly, but black knickers and bras should go together. Wear silky, lacy, sensual underwear and you will feel good about yourself, whatever you wear on top.

4. MUSIC   The deafening silence of singledom is not pleasant, so get into the habit of putting on music when you're alone. It can enhance your mood faster than any drug. Treat yourself to a stack of bargain CDs, and whatever your mood, you'll have suitable sounds for "Yeah! I'm Single," "No One Loves Me," and "But I'm Sexy Anyway."

5. CHAMPAGNE   I'm not advocating drinking alone (well, I occasionally might), but it's always helpful to have a bottle of champagne in the fridge. Like the emergency alarm on trains, it's nice to know it's there. You can open it after a terrible day, great news, or just on a wet weekend.

6. SILK SHEETS   For true sensuality you need one set of silk sheets. If there's no one to cuddle up to, wrapping your body in warm silk is the next best thing—and when there is, it's unlikely he'll complain either. However, don't take this to mean that anything warm and comforting is acceptable in bed. Grown women with a herd of stuffed animals on the pillow don't look like sexy bitches—they look scary.

7. CAT   While you're self-assured and independent, sometimes it's nice to someone to talk to. The perfect sexy bitch companion? A cat. Dogs are too much like men—messy, eager, and constantly in need of attention—whereas a cat simply slinks around, dispensing affection and warmth when it feels like it and wandering off to sleep when it doesn't.

8. HAIR   Just because you haven't got anyone to run fingers through your hair right now doesn't mean you should neglect it. To maintain your sexy bitch status, a great haircut is essential. Pay as much as you can afford and ask for a style that can easily be maintained. Well-groomed hair that looks healthy and touchable will make you feel gorgeous.

9. SHOES   Any girl can sex herself up with a pair of killer stilettos. They lengthen your legs, push out your butt, and make you walk like Marilyn— who, rumor has it, used to shave a little off one heel to give herself that sexy sway. To really go for it, invest in a pair of porn shoes—towering heels, ankle straps, and worn only by naked women who are about to bend over; these shoes are the ultimate in slut wear, but in a good way.

10. NEGLIGÉE   No one looks good in a chenille bathrobe—it ain't sexy. What you need is loungewear you see in Hollywood movies—sheer, almost-see-through negligée. It wisps around your body, drapes over your curves, and enhances your every movement. Get one in silk or satin, which warms to the temperature of your body, and slink around the house—the only problem will be bothering to get dressed at all.

even if it's just a selection of leaves in a frame. You can even hang your loveliest dress, scarf, or jewelry on the wall, to admire and inspire.

Also vital is lighting; harsh, overhead light is the bitter enemy of sensuality. Unless you're involved in painstaking surgical work or are searching for a lost earring, you don't actually need the relentless blaze of white overhead light. At least three lamps placed strategically around the room will create a comforting and attractive glow. Candles, too, make everyone look at least six times more attractive (I'm sure this is scientific fact) and twice as thin. Lava lamps, with their slow-moving, retro vibe, are ideal sensual lighting. Spotlights, which reveal every flaw no matter how well disguised, are not.

As for texture, if your furniture is looking less than perfect, invest in some throws made from fake fur or velvet. Obviously, you don't want the place to look like a bear trapper's cabin, so don't go overboard on the nylon wolf fur, but do think about texture as much as visual appeal. The bed will benefit from a pile of pillows and a velvet or satin bedspread, but if you have a penchant for dainty floral prints, do try and wean yourself off them. Sexy bitches don't live in a herbaceous border, on the whole.

If you have animals or you smoke, you'll need the air to smell a little nicer. Personally, I think air fresheners smell like the devil's panty liners and scented candles, real flowers and the old favorite sell-your-house smells of real coffee and baking bread (put a store-bought loaf in the oven—who'll know?) are far more sensual. If, like me, you're a bit of a slut, you may simply choose to disguise the dirty laundry with liberal sprays of expensive perfume, which also has the bonus of making your house smell like an eighteenth-century French whore's boudoir. And all you need then is a reasonable level of tidiness.

We're not talking anal neatness, just the sense that if you put something down, it won't immediately be obscured by dust bunnies and a top layer of mold. Basically, living like a sexy bitch is all about making your environment as desirable as you are. Which is, of course, very.

7

sexual fantasies

"Ever notice that 'what the hell' is always the right decision?"

—*Marilyn Monroe*

At the beginning of a relationship, sex is great, and that's without any props, aids, or spicing-up. But after a while, the old naked one-two starts to feel a little dull. At that point, any sexy bitch worth her salted Japanese cocktail snacks will do one of two things. She'll either leave him and go on to enjoy three energetic months with somebody new, or she'll introduce Fantasy Sex into the relationship and ensure that their lovemaking stays fresh, funky, and positively unforgettable for many more months, possibly even years, to come.

The truth is, everybody has sexual fantasies, and while some are for entirely private consumption only—the ones involving men who are sexier than your own, for example—there are plenty worth sharing. But getting the best result is simply the trick of knowing how to share them.

sharing fantasies

First rule: if you can't take the truth, don't ask the question. So if you're dying to ask, "Do you ever think about other women when we're having sex?" realize that there's at least a 50 percent chance the answer's going to be yes. And if he asks you (about men or women), weigh your answer carefully to avoid weeks of gloomy silences and hurt glances. While couples often smugly claim that they can tell each other anything, they're only smug because they don't know the half of it. Good fantasies to share are basic erotic ideas, or those that involve the two of you. Bad ones to mention are fantasies concerning others, such as ex-partners, family members, and best friends. It's not that there's anything wrong with a healthy fantasy life involving your boss and your man's brother, it's just that your man probably doesn't want to know about it.

That said, you can adapt almost any fantasy and make it palatable to share with him—it's a simple matter of taking it slowly, revealing a detail at a time, and leaving out the questionable dream lover.

Talking about your fantasies together means you get an insight into what turns each other on (and why). It also considerably boosts the chances that you'll actually get to enact them, if the same ideas turn you both on. Beginning the conversation, however, isn't always simple. Blurting out, "So, what are you thinking about?" at the point of orgasm won't allow him to open up gradually and sensitively. He's more likely to shout "tits!" and then regret it later. If you want to uncover his deepest desires, and reveal yours, the best way to instigate the discussion is while you're in bed, but still coherent. Perhaps a little stroking may take place to get you both in the mood, but anything more passionate makes it hard to talk.

Broach the topic with a question such as, "Do you ever think about doing it outside?" If he pulls away from you, horrified, and stammers, "But the police would lock us up," then perhaps don't take this any further. Any sort of encouraging response can lead to, "Where would you like to do it with me?" and "What exactly would we do?"

Before you know it, you're telling him exactly how you've always fantasized about having sex on the battlements of a windswept castle, dressed as Anne Boleyn—or whatever. When he tells you his own fantasies, don't say, "But that's so basic and dull." Most men don't have the same wild, flowery imaginations that women do. For them, a simple "she's wearing stockings" will generally suffice as a trigger, while women often like to create a cast of thousands entirely in period dress with a full script and a lighting technician before they can even begin to get turned on.

> **TIP**
>
> You can explore your wildest fantasies with role-play, even though in real life you'd run a mile from a sweaty biker, a horny doctor, or even an overeager intern at the office. You might find it fun to swap your usual roles, from the one being seduced to the seducer, for example.

dressing up and role-play

Once you've established the ideas that work for both of you, you might like to put them into practice. Not really hiking up to the battlements, silly; we're talking about role-play, the art of pretending. It used to be called "playing," but we're all adults now.

Role-play is a fantastic way to add a new dimension to your sex life. It can offer all the benefits of infidelity without any of the guilt or pain. All you need to do is decide on your fantasy roles (you can swap them at any time). Collect together an adult costume box, containing such items as hats, scarves, a feather boa, spectacles, or even a nurse's outfit. Let your imagination run free, but remember, often you only need one item to suggest a role—you don't need a full drama department.

A basic script helps, but get too involved in back story and motivation. A few lines of dialogue to get you in the mood will do. Try "Oh no, my car's broken down" (though not if you're being Anne Boleyn), "I feel so warm, I can't think why," "Where exactly does it hurt, sir?" and so on.

Good role-plays with strong dramatic parts for both of you include teacher and pupil, nurse/doctor and patient, businessman/woman and interviewee, lady/master of the manor and servant, and damsel in distress and helpful stranger. If you're filming it, use a tripod and try not to laugh; also, remember not to spend too long chatting and adjusting your costume. The whole point is to have sex, and role-play often helps couples to shed their inhibitions faster than a bottle of vodka will, because you're only acting, so you can say and do whatever you want.

back-door sex

How far you go sexually is, of course, entirely up to you. But the genuine sexy bitch has a fairly full repertoire, purely because it makes life interesting. And if you never try it, how do you know whether you'll like it or not?

One area of experimentation that never used to be mentioned but is now regularly discussed is anal sex. Men generally love it because it's a very tight fit and it's thoroughly dirty (in the sexual sense that is). Often women aren't so hot to try it because, for them, it's mainly painful and they worry that it's going to be dirty in an entirely different sense. Some women find the whole idea unnerving, and it's certainly a type of sex that depends on trust. They may feel degraded or distressed by the sheer physical intimacy of it, and if so, it's important to talk first. If you're doing it as a gesture of love, make sure he knows that, or he may expect a night of filthy passion and you'll be weeping into the pillow.

Ironically, men have a prostate gland up their anus, which produces pleasingly erotic sensations when stimulated. Women, sadly, do not. So the pleasure of anal sex is largely the mental excitement generated by doing something "dirty," although some women do enjoy the sensation of fullness, particularly if they also have something (a finger, a vibrator) in their vagina at the same time.

If you decide to give anal a whirl, there are certain basic rules for making the experience as pleasant as possible. First, it helps if he hasn't got a massive penis—though don't point this out to him. Whatever size it is, you need a lot of lubrication around your anus and all over his penis, which will be wearing a condom. Anal skin tears very easily, so hello pain and infections if you aren't careful. You can get heavy-duty condoms for anal sex, though you might prefer to order them via the internet.

You should be very turned on first—it won't work from a standing start. Unless all your muscles are thoroughly relaxed, it'll just feel like someone trying to wedge a grapefruit into a keyhole. Once you're in the mood, the best position is doggy style. That way, he can see exactly what he's doing. He needs to enter you very, very slowly, one inch at a time. Make it clear before he begins to thrust that violent plunging is out; only gentle, slow thrusts are acceptable.

When he pulls out, he must not touch your vagina with his penis because bacteria can be transferred. Apart from that, you're fine. Anything you've heard about anal prolapse isn't true—you'd have to do it with an entire rugby team for three days straight to cause that kind of problem, and we all know you're not that kind of sexy bitch.

threesomes and orgies

This is where even the sexiest sexy bitch glances behind her in nervous, Scooby-Doo fashion, as she prepares to step further into the deserted ghost train that is threesomes and orgies. While they are the mainstay of porn and a hugely popular fantasy, the reality can be scarier than a whole bunch of skeletons. It's not that they aren't enjoyable—physically they can be great, which is why there are so many clubs and parties offering a modern take on the old 1970s sport of swinging—this time without the car keys and the droopy 'staches. But emotionally—well, hold on tight.

Recruiting someone else to have sex with you and your partner is like sticking your hand in a crocodile pit for the buzz. It might be exciting, but it can all end in disaster. If it's a female friend, there's the jealousy issue—is she better in bed than me? Has he always fantasized about her? Will he want her more than me? What if they start doing it behind my back? If it's a male friend, ditto for him. And if it's a stranger culled from the internet or a local swinger's club, you know nothing about that person, or their strange sexual diseases, or even, possibly, their loving partner and three kids back home.

Then there's the possibility that you'll like it too much and suddenly, two-person sex won't seem anything like as much fun. Or you'll fall in love with them or they'll fall in love with you, and you can never see them again without blowing your relationship sky-high. Of course, there is a slim possibility that you'll all have a great time sexually; remain healthy, mutually supportive adults throughout; and agree to do it every so often on special occasions, while happily returning to normalcy in between. And there's a possibility that the crocodile won't feel very hungry. But it's unlikely.

If you do go ahead, despite everything, always observe threesome etiquette, which states that no person must feel left out. Two people getting it on while another watches miserably from the sidelines is not a threesome, it's a floorshow. Wondering how to get started? Well, I'm tempted to say that if you can't get that far on your own, you probably shouldn't be attempting it at all. But if you're really stuck, try strip poker.

Oddly enough, orgies are actually a safer bet emotionally, if you can cope with the sight of your partner amid a writhing pit of nubile lovelies. Having said that, most swingers aren't that lovely, so if you are going to try it, you may want to investigate the possibility of joining a very exclusive, members-only club that only permits beautiful people to swing. Otherwise you may be stuck with Over-35s Night at Xanadu Blue, above the Chinese takeout.

Of course, if you are going to swing, never, ever, swing in any direction without a condom and never do anything you feel unsure about, just because your partner swears it's his (or her) greatest fantasy. Let them keep it as a fantasy and then you retain your self-respect and mental wholeness. You're a sexy bitch, remember, not a sex toy.

sadomasochism and bondage

S&M is about giving and receiving pain, domination, and submission. But the roster of experiences that fall under that heading range from a mild tap on the bottom to being hung from a hook and ritually flogged by a gimp-masked master. Most of us don't want to go as far as that, but that doesn't mean we don't want to experiment, trying on the sub (submissive) and dom (dominant) personas for size.

> **TIP**
>
> Bondage requires trust, particularly trust that he isn't going to step out for a drink while you're tied up.

Sadists get turned on by inflicting pain, while masochists enjoy receiving it. But that doesn't mean you can't swap if you're not sure which one works for you. For some, there's a thin line between pain and pleasure. The nerves are stimulated by both and if your brain makes a connection between pain and excitement, this can quickly translate into desire. There are basic elements to S&M, so if you're interested, read on—you may as well do it right, rather than attempting a flogging with a bent coathanger and wondering why it's not much fun.

leather, rubber, and other clothing

S&M clothes are all about power, so black is usually the color of choice. Skintight PVC and leather are also popular, as is specially constructed underwear hung with chains and studs. The erotic ideas of restraint and bondage are usually apparent, too, and shiny high heels are obligatory, the more kitten-skewering the better. Blindfolds are also useful, but you can improvise with silk scarves. Fetish shops stock entire departments, from lacy bustiers to studded and buckled helmets, so your particular sartorial fantasy shouldn't be hard to find. Some S&Mers swear by leather, because it has the feel of warm skin and the smell can be erotic. Others prefer the modern stretch of PVC, while still more insist that rubber is the only true S&M clothing. Whether you want jackboots and a studded pouch, or a high-heels-and-stockings combo, you can adapt your favorite parts of the S&M look and discard the rest. Fetish wear generally makes women—particularly sexy bitches—look tall, thin, and menacingly powerful, which can only be a good thing.

props and accessories

The committed S&Mer may have an enormous box of tricks dedicated purely to hanging, strapping, thrashing, and slapping. However, for the weekend amateur—or the sexy bitch who just wants to spice up her life—there are only a few basics required. The chief accessory is a set of handcuffs, and the fluffy versions are much more comfortable. The main points to remember are: whatever you do, don't lose the key, and don't leave anyone handcuffed to anything for long, or they'll faint from restricted blood flow.

The most comfortable "cuffed" position is with the hands in front of the body, but if that's not bondage-porn enough for you both, you can cuff your partner to a piece of furniture (like the bed). If you're lying down, avoid cuffing behind the back; hands stuck underneath the bottom is unpleasant, rather than arousing.

If handcuffs seem a little hard core, use bondage tape (often available from sex shops in black or pink), which unpeels easily but does the job. You can gag each other if you want, but never put anything tight around someone's neck. You may also wish to invest in a small whipping device. A leather cat-o'-nine tails is good, because it provides the requisite swishing noise, feels suitably naughty when whacked against bare buttocks, and looks the part. You can buy a full whip, but it's difficult to wield accurately and the danger is that you might do infinitely more damage than you ever intended to. There's always the riding crop option (and they provide a pretty good slap), but again this can be agonizing if wielded harshly. Order a few types from the internet and send back the scariest—or keep them, depending on your point of view.

Nipple clamps and similar accessories are also an option. Today you can have any part of your body pierced, clamped, electrified, or be hung, and S&Mers frequently do. If you are considering this, make sure you go to a reputable piercing establishment. Do your research thoroughly first, too—if you don't like it, it's too late once you've had a metal post shot through your clitoris.

lessons in safety

Of course, when you're incorporating pain, bondage, and helplessness into your sex games, there's always a danger that, shall we say, something can go wrong. If you're mid role-play and shout, "No, stop!" (Or "Ffo! fffop!" if you happen to be gagged at the time), there's every chance your partner will simply assume you're throwing yourself into character, and continue on regardless. That's why S&M fans have a "safe word," which can be used only in the context of "end the game now" or "stop what you're doing." The word is usually something thoroughly incongruous, like "teapot."

TOP TEN SEXY-BITCH PROPS

1. LEATHER GLOVES Texturally exciting for stroking and hand jobs, leather gloves also add dangerous frisson to S&M sexual encounters.

2. HANDCUFFS Try the fluffy ones, or the silk-lined if you prefer, and make sure you can lock and unlock them easily. The metal policeman's kind can bite unpleasantly, but you might find that exciting.

3. VIBRATOR Every sexy bitch should have one. Work out what you want it for—clitoris, vagina, penis-substitute, double penetration with his penis, or simply a gentle buzzing sensation—and supplement your box of delights with as many types as you like.

4. LUBE A bedroom (or elsewhere) essential, a tube of lubrication is needed when foreplay just isn't doing the trick, you're tired and stressed, or you're experimenting with some anal sex (see page 85). Just a drop will be enough to replicate your natural secretions and it's more pleasant if you warm it in your palms first. You can also use it to ease your hand jobs—it'll speed them up remarkably.

5. VIDEO CAMERA Cheaper technology means that anyone can make their own private porn film. Get a tripod, press "record," and away you go. And if you want to make a Victorian porn film, simply turn the dial to "sepia" for a strangely erotic time-travel experience. Make sure you've agreed on everything with your partner first (see page 94) or you might end up showing all to the world.

Both S&M and bondage require a high level of trust, and anyone who's ever been sexually or emotionally abused should be particularly careful. What's a fun power game to one person can easily be a

6. STILETTOS We've already established the pros of high heels but for S&M they're essential to establish the power divide—no, not on him, he can just wear big boots. For you, they're sex armor, and the spikier the better.

7. CAT-O'-NINE TAILS A flicky sort of whip that swishes appealingly across the butt without leaving too much agony in its wake. Also looks excellent with any form of PVC cat-woman costume you dare wear. What do you mean, you haven't got a sewing machine?

8. CORSET Restraint, fetishism, and a tiny waist—you'll have it all with a corset. It's true sexy-bitch wear. Few men can resist the erotic symbolism of tightly laced breasts and waist. Whether you keep it on for sex, or let him untie you first, it's worth the hassle of lacing it up in the first place.

9. PADDLE Small hitting devices, which resemble ping-pong bats, are ideal for the sadist who doesn't like to get her hands sore. Paddles enable effective bottom slapping from a short distance and make the job much easier because your arms won't get as tired—though his bottom might.

10. SILK SCARVES Easier to untie than ropes, tape, and handcuffs, silk scarves are fail-safe bondage equipment. They undo very easily, they feel sensual, and they also double up as blindfolds. Every home should have at least two, but make sure they haven't got nylon in them or the knots will never come undone.

damaging reminder of a painful past experience to another. Make sure you are happy with what's going on at all times, don't allow anyone you don't know and trust thoroughly to tie you up, and if you feel uncomfortable, say so immediately. The idea is to get turned on, not to lie there praying for him to come and undo the knots. And, of course, one-night stands are not the time to put yourself in a position of vulnerability. And if your new lover seems just a little too eager to slap you in handcuffs, you may want to wonder why.

exhibitionism and voyeurism

Exhibitionists like to reveal themselves, or get caught, having sex. For them, the thrill comes from being viewed. So if you're a sexy bitch who happens to be an exhibitionist, you need to make sure you don't get arrested—or, worse, assaulted. Walking around half naked is out, as is having sex in front of the window, which could cause passers-by some trouble. Find a way to demonstrate your desires safely.

Outdoor sex can be relatively safe, but it's illegal in many countries and can count as public obscenity. Well, you may think you're a thing of beauty and a joy forever, but the policeman might disagree.

So if you do crave risky exhibitionist sex choose a deserted beach or a secluded park rather than a nightclub dance floor, and an empty alleyway over a main road. You still get the buzz of knowing someone might see you, but it's less likely, at least. It is also essential to know the legal restrictions of the country you are in, or your perfect romantic adventure might land you in prison. The other, more failsafe, way to indulge your exhibitionism is to film yourselves making love—or just alone, stripping or masturbating. That way, your lovemaking won't be seen by anyone but you, though you will still get the excitement of seeing yourself on-screen and you can even pretend you're turning on the entire nation. If you really want to, you can send your film to one of the porn companies specializing in "real couples"—and just hope your parents aren't racier than you thought when it comes to spicing up their own love life via mail-order video. If you go this route, consider drawing up a contract that prevents your partner from posting you in all your glory on the internet or distributing your image to his 500 closest friends. If you're in any doubt, you can consult an attorney for advice on making it legal and binding.

For voyeurs, life is more difficult (isn't it always?), because watching other people without their knowledge is, naturally enough, a criminal offense. However, there are private clubs that allow voyeurs to meet exhibitionists—now there's a match made in heaven—and watch them writhe around. But if that's too scary, the internet is just bursting with web-cam couples dying to be watched, though make sure it's a secure site and they're not going to get your financial details and swipe your bank account. Be careful, too, not to follow any questionable links involving "young and sexy" girls or the police might make a questionable link to you.

sex toys

Strictly speaking, sex toys aren't all that experimental, given that nowadays a good 50 percent of women own one. But they're definitely worth including in your sexy-bitch repertoire—and not just for times when your boyfriend's out of town. One vibrator is fine, but there are so many shapes and sizes available, it's more fun to have a few. A good selection would be a normal seven-inch three-speed. This is good for holding against your clitoris when he's inside you, and can also buzz pleasantly against the shaft of his penis. Then you need a waterproof toy for shower- and bath-based sex—a good model is I Rub My Duckie, which is—as you'd suspect—a vibrator cunningly disguised as a rubber duck. You could also use the cock-ring/vibrating-attachment sort, which is a soft rubber ring that fits round the base of his penis with a projecting section of nodules that lie against your clitoris, providing a constant buzz as he grinds away—so convenient. You could also choose a lipstick-shaped one that you can discreetly carry in your bag—or the old classic Rabbit vibrator with all the jiggling balls, for those times when your orgasm is all that matters.

Then there are the more esoteric toys—the anal beads, for example, which you place up his bottom (use lubrication at this point, and don't argue) and whip out at the moment of orgasm to stimulate his prostate. Or the Tongue Joy, which slips over the tongue to sex up oral with an extra buzz. The best way to choose the ingredients of your personal sexy-bitch toy box is to take a tour of the sex shop websites or go in person to the new, increasingly female-friendly sex shops (see Resources on page 116).

8 sexual troubles

"When choosing between two evils I always pick the one I never tried before."

—*Mae West*

Now you've bravely ploughed through the entire book. By this time, you'll know how to ensnare a man at 50 paces and exactly what to do when you've got him. You'll know how to dress, how to move and what to say to take your rightful place as a qualified sexy bitch. But there's just one problem and it's this: all the technical knowledge, attitude, and beauty in the world will not give you a great sex life if you and your partner can't communicate.

Communication is the lifeblood of good sex; without it you can run through a repertoire of bedroom tricks that would startle a Bangkok hooker and nothing will flicker but the bedside light. Of course, most relationships start off with the paths of communication running smoothly and congestion-free. But as time goes by, life gets in the way of love, and work, tiredness, kids, socializing, bills, and even DIY and TV begin to replace those hours you once spent sharing every last thought and emotion that passed through your mind. Admittedly, it may have been a pain for everyone else, but for you and him it was bliss. Once those days are gone and you've thrown in a hefty sprinkling of resentment, unresolved annoyance, daily irritations, jealousy, and marital martyrdom, it's a wonder you ever want to have sex at all. When you do, it's often perfunctory, because no one wants to appear vulnerable or to voice all the issues that remain under the carpet. Even if it is loving, it can still be basic, because you're exhausted and you've both got to get an early start the next morning.

No wonder communication suffers. And if sex is just a pale shadow of what it used to be, it's unlikely that your bodies have changed, or you've unaccountably forgotten how to touch each other. It's much more feasible that you've forgotten how to talk to each other and that's why you've both lost that lovin' feeling (and it's gone, gone, gone…whooo-ooh-ooh).

And then there are the other sexual problems the ones nobody likes to talk about at all, however good their communication skills might be—such as sexually transmitted diseases (STDs). Or the constant hassle of finding a form of contraception that works and doesn't ruin sex or your mood. In fact, it's a wonder anyone has good sex at all, when you think about it. But they do, and so can you, with some inside information.

how to communicate

Without "emotional intelligence" you can't be a sexy bitch. The term is simply a fancy description for empathy—the ability to understand how someone else is feeling and recognize your own feelings for what they are. We all know that depression is often unexpressed anger and that anger is frequently a disguise for fear, but remembering it when we're about to throw a plate at his head is the hard part.

So if communication has broken down to the point where sex seems an unwelcome intrusion into your life, the first thing you need to do is to sit down together to talk and listen. Built-up resentment between you usually means that one person expresses how they feel while the other interrupts, and the whole thing can end in a shower of recriminations and abuse, so you need to borrow a few tricks from relationship therapy.

To ensure that you both have a fair chance to talk without interruption, set a time limit during which one person speaks and the other is not permitted to interrupt, and then it's the other person's turn. (Use an egg timer, so no one cheats.) Try not to make wild, sweeping generalizations such as "you always" and "you never." Instead, try to restrict your explanations to how you feel. For example, rather than saying, "You make me upset when…" accept that being upset is your own response and say, "I feel upset when I feel unheard" or something similar. Take the accusation out of the sentence and it is much easier to hear. You can also check that you've understood what you're being told by repeating his words back to him. Otherwise it's very tempting only to hear what you assume he's saying, and not the reality.

If your communication problems are largely confined to sex, take the pressure off by discussing them outside the bedroom. Practical sex problems are much easier to resolve than emotional issues, but both will be eased by communicating effectively. So if you don't like what he does in bed, remember that the golden rule is "four pieces of praise to one piece of negativity." Slot "It hurts me when you get too rough and I don't like it" in among "You're such a good kisser" and "I love being in bed with you." Try not to sound carping or weary. Imagine how you'd like to be asked to change your sexual behavior and adapt your tone accordingly.

If he's criticizing you, ask yourself whether he has a point, but never accept personal abuse or cruelty. Anything he says should be asked or offered from a position of his loving you and wanting to improve your relationship. If you're not sure, ask yourself this question: "If my best friend's boyfriend spoke to her like that, would I think he was being reasonable or would I regard him as a brute?" Most women, even sexy bitches, have a tendency to get down on themselves, so don't aid and abet a bully by checking your self-esteem at the door.

If your communication problems seem too severe to overcome, sexually or otherwise, consider counseling. Try couples therapy or one-on-one. While this may not make a silk purse out of a sow's ear, it can be invaluable in helping you to decide whether to stay or go. In healthy relationships, most issues can be resolved with a cunning combination of listening and compromising—just make sure you're not the only one doing either.

what happens if you lose interest in sex?

Few women are constantly sex-mad. Hormones, periods, pregnancy, stress, and tiredness can mess with female sex drive as effectively as nuclear testing messes with nature. Occasionally losing interest in sex doesn't mean that you're not a sexy bitch, just that you're normal. But the real problem arises when you lose interest permanently. The likeliest explanation is simply that your feelings for your partner have changed and your sex drive will return in full flower when you meet someone new.

> **TIP**
>
> Sometimes taking the pressure off having sex can help restore sex drive. Just cuddle; it doesn't have to lead anywhere.

Other issues to look at include body image, both yours and his. For example, if he has recently stopped exercising or has displayed visible signs of aging, he may feel less desirable and therefore stop making approaches. His altered appearance may also put you off, albeit subconsciously.

Equally, if you don't feel good about yourself, you won't feel like a sexy bitch, and every time you get naked, you'll be obsessing about your flab instead of enjoying the sensations and the closeness. Unfortunately, the media plays a large part in suggesting that no one can possibly be worth making love to unless they weigh less than a gnat and have a stomach you could bounce dried peas off.

But good sex has been continuing for many millennia, and flat stomachs are merely an obsession of the last few decades. The human race has not died out yet, so it stands to reason that people found each other sexually attractive even when they had missing teeth, tanning only happened in leather workshops, and they were sewn into their winter underwear with no chance of a bath until next spring. So all you modern-day sexy bitches out there, remember just how desirable you are. Of course, if you are ill, exhausted, stressed and tense, or suffering from PMS, no one expects you to be having sex, though if you try it, you might surprise yourself. Then again, you might sometimes be happier simply being left in a corner with a box of chocolates and a video of *Breakfast at Tiffany's*—and who could blame you?

Sometimes, nothing you do helps you feel like having sex. If that's the case, you may be suffering from a deeper malaise, such as depression or even a hormonal imbalance. If your libido has packed its bags and gone away, seemingly for good, it's worth going to see the doctor. Unless your partner's suddenly put on lots of weight and refuses to wash, of course, in which case your lack of desire is perfectly understandable.

top ten sexual worries

Sexual worries can ruin your life—but they don't need to. Nowadays it's easier than ever to get help, whether via the internet, books, or magazines, or just by talking to friends. There are clinics dedicated to sexual health that will not, I promise, judge you, and psychotherapists who specialize in sexual issues. So you don't need to suffer in silence.

1. CAN'T COME, WON'T COME If you simply cannot orgasm, it's far more likely to be due to emotional, rather than physical, reasons. You may be scared of sex, afraid to let go and appear vulnerable, or you have learned from your upbringing that nice girls "don't." Talk to your man, let him know just how patient he has to be, and consider counseling. If masturbation doesn't work, it could be a physical problem and you'd benefit from seeing a doctor. Some women suffer from vaginismus, a condition where the vaginal muscles freeze to prevent entry. This does not mean you're frigid, just that you may need therapy to get to the root of the problem.

2. THE CONDOM QUESTION   "I didn't know how to mention it" is not a good excuse when you're suffering from a sexual disease that you could have avoided if only you'd used a condom. Deep down, all men know they should use one—and if he seems dismissive, doesn't mention it, or, worse, refuses to have sex wearing one, then you really need to make it clear. Carry your own, don't rely on him, and make sure they're accessible at the crucial moment. A selection of different varieties to choose from can make wearing one a tiny bit more appealing. A calm "I never have sex without one" should do the trick—and if not, ask yourself if you really want this man.

3. HE WANTS THINGS I DON'T   If he's pressuring you to indulge in sexual practices that you hate, ask yourself what's going on. Do you dislike what he's suggesting because someone told you it was bad, or because you genuinely know it's not for you? If it's the latter, any decent guy will drop the subject once you've given him an outright "no." However, if your reluctance extends to sex in any position but missionary and you have an aversion to blowjobs, then it's not entirely his fault, and you may both benefit from couples counseling.

4. HE WANTS IT MORE THAN ME   Mismatched sexual appetites are a serious problem for many couples. But as Woody Allen says in *Annie Hall*, "She never wants sex—maybe two, three times a week," while Diane Keaton sighs, "We do it all the time—twice a week at least." So it's as much about perception as frequency. You may both have to compromise—let him take sexy pictures of you and masturbate over them, or give him a hand job instead, while he must accept the fact that daily sex is a rare occurrence in most relationships, at least past the first month.

5. HE THINKS ABOUT HIS EX/PORN   Insensitivity is the enemy of good sex, not to mention good communication. So if he likes to remember the hot time he had with his ex, or to remark on how stunning some babe walking down the street looks, he's committing the cardinal sin of relationships. Sexually speaking, this should be the bottom line: unless specifically asked, he should never refer to a previous partner's sexual habits. And of course, neither should you. If he does, say, "Well, that was then, this is now," and let him know that you find the gory details off-putting and unsexy. That should shut him up.

6. SMALL PENIS   A penis that's genuinely classed as a micro is under two inches, so I bet it's not that bad. The average for Caucasian guys is about six inches. For Asians, five inches, and for African-Americans, seven inches. And it's more or less true that it's what you do with it that counts. However, if it's very thin or short, you may have trouble enjoying all the wonderful sensations of sex. There's very little he can do about it, so be kind. Close your thighs when he enters you to narrow your vagina and squeeze your internal muscles around his penis—this is guaranteed to make a thin penis feel wider and it will increase the friction, and the resulting intensity of feeling, for the both of you. Remember, you have nerve endings in only the first three inches anyway, so as long as he can thrust, you can still have a good time.

7. HE'LL THINK I'M TARTY   Plenty of women, sexy bitches included, are convinced that if they talk about their true desires, their men will leave them for someone more traditional. Women are still afraid of being seen as "whores" if they want any kind of experimental sex that falls outside the normal boundaries of what "nice girls do." It's important to remember that you have just as much right as any man to state what turns you on, and to ask your man to fulfill your desires. Bed is the place where you can truly be yourself and if you feel you can't, it may not be your needs that are wrong, but your man's attitude. Although if you're demanding that he dress up as your ex-boyfriend, his reluctance may be understandable. He's sensitive too, so go easy on him.

8. PREMATURE EJACULATION If the problem is two strokes and you're out, he may be suffering from premature ejaculation. He may be too excited, too nervous, or too inexperienced to hold on (see page 60 for techniques to calm him down). If the suggested methods don't work, it may be a symptom of a psychological problem, in which case he'll benefit from seeing a psychosexual counselor to discuss his feelings about sex.

9. NEVER HAVE TIME FOR SEX Life has a tendency to overwhelm your desire to have sex, and suddenly, by the time you've staggered through everything else you have to do, the very idea of having any time left over for it seems insane. In that case, you need to book time, just as you would for a meeting or a gym class. It may sound heartless and unromantic, but what's romantic about never having sex at all? Pencil in, for example, a Friday night, take a bottle of wine to bed, and get down to it. You'll feel ten times better and you can make it a regular date in the future.

10. BORED WITH SEX What if you are still attracted to him and still like him, but you just can't be bothered to have sex anymore? Basically, you've slipped into a rut and your libido has died. But it's not the end; there are ways to revive it, chief of which is to get out of the house. Our environment plays a much bigger part in sex than we realize and one night in a hotel room, away from all the demands of bills, kids, and dirty laundry, can do wonders. Or try music, candlelight, and a picnic on the living room floor (but don't switch on the TV). Buy new underwear, invest in a vibrator, and try to rekindle your desire by thinking about what attracted you to him in the first place. With sex, it's a case of use it or lose it.

sexual diseases

The fastest growth in STDs (sexually transmitted diseases), also known as STIs (sexually transmitted infections), is currently among young women, which suggests we're being a little less careful than we once were. Nobody's judging the number of sexual partners you may have had (or what you do with them), but whoever you sleep with, whether it's one man a year, 17 a week, or just your husband, unless you have conclusive proof that they are not carriers or have never suffered any sexually transmitted diseases, you'd be insane not to insist on using a condom.

A few mild suggestions in the first two weeks of your relationship, followed by a drunken night of passion when you're sure it's safe and after which you don't bother any more, does not count as protecting your sexual health. Condoms are better than they used to be; they're thinner and more sensitive. Compare them with a month of discharge, uncomfortable itches, and the abject terror that you've caught something unmentionable.

The good news is that as long as you're prepared to go and be examined, nearly all STDs can be cured with antibiotics or a painless procedure. But if you refuse to face up to your symptoms, you may risk such illnesses as pelvic inflammatory disease (PID), which can lead to infertility, not to mention the risk of passing it on to your partner and possibly all his future partners.

Needless to say, if you're having sex with a guy whose penis is not looking all that great—cracked skin, discharge, or even spots—the chances are he's already contracted an STD and you should avoid him like the plague. However, many men are apparently symptomless, or they may have had something once and now are just a carrier, which means they can pass it on without showing any signs themselves. With a new partner, it's always hard to tell—and he may not know that he's a carrier. Which is why you should continue using condoms for at least six months and up to two years, which gives most diseases a chance to develop. If he's been exposed to HIV or hepatitis C, then he must get tested regardless.

The following categories are the chief STDs to look out for and what to expect if you think you've got one. But don't rely on this list to diagnose yourself: every sensible sexy bitch makes a friend of her gynecologist or her local family-planning/women's health clinic, and will visit at the first irritating itch.

chlamydia

Over half of those infected have no symptoms. In women, the bacteria affects your cervix and if you do show symptoms they may include yellowish discharge, bleeding or spotting between periods, and pain when you urinate. This is a disease you must tackle, or it can lead to pelvic inflammatory disease (PID). Antibiotics can be used to treat chlamydia, but you may have infected your partner(s), so you'll need to tell them too. Not fun, but essential.

crabs

The familiar term for pubic lice, crabs are passed around in a way similar to head lice, only via pubic hair. They are visible and, although harmless, very itchy and unpleasant. Crabs can be treated with a special shampoo but the itching may remain for up to two weeks after they've gone.

cystitis

Although not sexually transmitted, cystitis is an inflammation of the bladder and/or urethra, often caused by rough sex, and is sometimes referred to as "honeymoon" cystitis. The symptoms are a sensation of burning when you urinate, cloudy urine and the frequent need to pee, but then nothing happening when you get there. Drink plenty of water and cranberry juice, which is good for your bladder, but if it's really bad you'll need antibiotics to clear it up.

gonorrhea

This is also known as "the clap." Women seldom display severe symptoms, but if you do, they resemble those of chlamydia, while men get soreness and discharge. This is one STD that can lead to pelvic inflammatory disease (PID) and infertility, so if you suspect you're at risk, you must take antibiotics and inform your partner of your situation. As with any sexually transmitted disease, do not have unprotected sex until your treatment is completed and the infection is cleared up.

herpes

Symptoms include blisters on your genitals, which will burst and form ulcers. The first attack can involve flulike symptoms and the blisters will be sore. Unfortunately, there's no cure; once the virus is in your bloodstream, it will lie dormant and recur occasionally. However, it can be managed, but you must visit a specialist. Avoid sex when the virus is active and use creams and antiviral drugs to minimize discomfort. After the first outbreak, future ones are generally much milder.

HIV

Lately, young men and women have become less fearful of contracting HIV (human immunodeficiency virus). The mass panic of the 1980s has become more of an afterthought for the next generation—but it shouldn't have. It's now spreading faster among straight women than gay men (because gay men got the condom message). The virus attacks immune cells in the body and quickly mutates, which means that normal infections can take hold and eventually develop into AIDS (acquired immunodeficiency syndrome). Modern drugs vastly improve the life expectancy and quality of life for sufferers, but the simplest way to avoid it is to use a condom.

syphilis

The disease of nineteenth-century Paris has returned and is thoroughly unpleasant. You're unlikely to catch it, but just in case, symptoms include an initial genital ulcer, which enters your bloodstream and leads to further outbreaks. In turn, this damages the immune system and, finally, the heart and brain. It can be cured via muscle-injected antibiotics; left untreated, it can kill you, so don't casually ignore that weeping genital ulcer, will you?

trichomoniasis vaginalis

This infection is due to a parasitical bacterium and results in a greenish discharge, an unpleasant fishy smell, and soreness and burning around the vulva. Sometimes there are no apparent symptoms. Again, antibiotics can cure it.

warts

Caused by the human papilloma virus, genital warts are small cauliflower-shaped growths around the labia and vagina. You catch them through contact with infected skin and they may take up to two years to develop. The warts can be treated with a chemical cream or frozen off.

yeast infection

This is an infection of the candidiasis fungus, which can overpower your natural bacteria and cause symptoms that include itching, soreness around your vagina, and a thick whitish discharge. It is not usually related to sex, though it can be spread via this route, including oral sex. Topical creams and suppositories, available over the counter at the drugstore, are the usual cure.

Contraception

There are so many forms of contraception available, you'd think remaining baby-free would be a simple matter. However, nature wants you to get pregnant, so the only way to avoid its wishes is to be absolutely efficient when it comes to using your chosen method of contraception. Having it on the shelf will not prevent you from getting pregnant, nor will carrying it in your purse. If you don't read the instructions, in nine months' time you'll be a sexy bitch with a screaming bundle. Reading through the following options will help you to discover the method that suits your lifestyle, and your partner, best. Consult a medical professional for further advice.

cap/diaphragm

Like condoms, these work via the barrier method, so they don't mess around with your hormones. Both versions fit inside your vagina, covering your cervix so that sperm can't penetrate. Diaphragms are rubber domes, but caps are generally smaller and made from silicone. The upside is that you can put them in place well before sex, so there are no interruptions, and they can stay in for a while afterward. However, you have to use them with spermicide, which can be messy, and they can be awkward to fit and take out. They will need to be refitted if your weight changes by more than ten pounds, and if you give birth. You will also need to inspect them for tiny holes and get them replaced periodically.

the coil/intrauterine device

The coil, or IUD, is a little copper and plastic device that is fitted into your womb by highly trained professionals. It has a thread attached, which remains at the top of your vagina and it can stay in place for three to ten years. Coils aren't generally recommended if you haven't had a child, and they can cause pain and heavy periods, but if you want a nonhormonal form of contraception that you can forget about, it's worth considering.

coitus interruptus

Otherwise known as "getting off the stop before," this involves the man pulling out before he ejaculates. All I can say is, that's how I got pregnant. Not a reliable method by any means.

condom/femidom

Condoms are remarkably simple yet effective—they stop the sperm entering your body and keep it all in a little bag. The downside is that you have to halt what you're doing, grope around for the package, take care not to rip the plastic open; he may lose his erection, the light gets switched on, and, eventually, you wonder why you're bothering. Still, they do work and, most vitally, they protect you from STDs.

As for the Femidom, I've never met anyone who's used it more than once, because it's like sticking a hooped crinoline up your vagina. But, like the condom, it is highly effective against pregnancy and STDs.

contraceptive implants

Small flexible tubes are placed under the skin of your arm and release progesterone from year to year. Norplant and Implanon are currently available. Norplant is effective for five years and Implanon for three. Again, this is ideal if you're trekking through Borneo with no access to a drugstore, but there are reports of unpleasant side-effects and many women have had them removed well before the time is up.

depo provera

This is the progestogen-only injection, a long-term method that's ideal for the forgetful woman. Depo Provera (the most common type) protects you for up to three months, however there can be side effects such as mild depression. Because the hormone is injected into the muscle and is slowly released, you can't get rid of it for the entire time it's in you, so be very sure before you decide to take it.

morning-after pill

If you've had a condom break (which is doubtless what you'll tell the nurse, even if you were just drunk and forgot to use anything), you can get emergency contraception from the morning-after pill. They are actually two pills, and contain a massive dose of hormones, which you take 12 hours apart. Chances are that you'll feel very sick. You can take them up to 72 hours after sex, but don't make a habit of it—it's really not good for you. In some countries it is available at pharmacies or from a general practitioner.

the pill: combined

Containing the hormones progestogen and estrogen, the Combined Pill stops your ovaries from releasing an egg every month, and it thickens your cervical mucus. It also thins your womb lining, making it much harder to accept a fertilized egg. Many women swear by the Pill because it is a nonintrusive barrier method. But if you're over 35, or a smoker, it's not a wise move—it can raise your blood pressure and increase the risk of a stroke, among other problems.

the pill: mini

The progestogen-only pill contains a hormone similar to one naturally produced in the ovaries. It's a milder dose than the Combined Pill because it simply thickens your cervical mucus to prevent an egg from turning up unannounced. However, it's also slightly less reliable and you have to have a good memory because you're supposed to take it at the same time every day.

rhythm method

Beloved of hippies and Catholics, the rhythm method is noninterventionist and based on nature's cycles, which is why so many of its devotees have at least six children. In an ideal world, however, it works by teaching you to recognize your fertile and infertile times, by logging your temperature daily when you wake up and by understanding your cervical secretions—as if you've nothing better to do—and understanding the pattern of your menstrual cycle. There are electronic fertility devices, such as Persona, which can help, and these have you urinate on sticks of paper and enter in data about your cycle. But, really, isn't it easier just to use a condom?

After your period, you may notice a few days when you feel dry. No cervical secretions will be seen or felt. Then the secretions produced by your cervix change in texture and increase in amount. At first, they feel moist, sticky and white or cloudy. This is the start of the fertile time. The secretions then become clearer, wetter, stretchy and slippery, like raw egg white. This is a sign that you are ovulating and at your most fertile.

Afterword

Congratulations! You are now a fully-fledged sexy bitch, ready to hit the world with your charm, grace, and sensuality. Be aware, however, that everyone has off days. No one feels like a sexy bitch all the time; no one acts like one the whole time. But you can still use your inner sexy bitch as a guide to how you should feel about yourself. All women deserve to feel desirable, confident, and loved. Keep telling yourself that you are, keep acting as though you are, and you've pretty much got it made. And if someone you love keeps telling you differently, it's their problem, not yours. The single most important thing for any sexy bitch to remember is that she's worth it. Don't let anyone bring you down, because you deserve only the best, from life, love—and, of course, sex.

resources

Bibibaby
www.bibibaby.com

A dating site for bi-curious women to meet similarly minded woman to talk to, on- or offline.

Cake
www.cakenyc.com

An entertainment company dedicated to providing education and information about female sexual culture. The website is a resource for exploring female sexuality, pleasure, health, and politics.

The Clitoris
www.the-clitoris.com

Practical information is given on anatomy, female desire and fantasy, sex techniques, health, and more. Choose to read in English, French, Spanish, or German.

Cliterati
www.cliterati.co.uk

A fantasy site for women featuring sex news, health, articles, reviews, and shopping.

The Erotic Review
www.theeroticreview.co.uk

The site gives subscription and content info on this literary erotic magazine, which contains essays, interviews, features, and fiction by leading authors and journalists.

Female First
www.femalefirst.co.uk

An online magazine for women. The "Are You Feeling Naughty?" section features advice on romance, talking dirty, breaking up, sexual problems, sexual positions, erotic stories, and fantasies and sex toys.

Good Vibrations
www.goodvibes.com

This San Francisco Bay area institution has been serving the public since 1977. The online store carries sex toys, lubes, condoms, erotic books and guides, videos and DVDs, and more. The online magazine has erotica, advice columns, and interesting articles.

Lady Bliss
www.ladybliss.com

Lady Bliss' online store supplies lingerie, sex toys, romance enhancers, and erotic books and DVDs. The site also hosts erotica and sexual health information.

Libida
www.libida.com

Based in California, Libida is a unique, safe, and stimulating website where women can purchase adult products and "explore their sexuality in a positive and imaginative way." An online store for sex toys, erotic books, and DVDs, the site also features an "ask the sexperts" column, a "how to" section, lovemaking tips, health issues, and articles and erotica by celebrated writers and artists.

Masturbate for Peace
www.masturbateforpeace.com

The site urges visitors to replace negative feelings, which cause conflict, with love, particularly self-love, and to join together to masturbate for peace—to share masturbation's positive energy with a world in need. The site also offers a sex toy shopping boutique, poetry, pictures, and further masturbation resources.

Nerve magazine
www.nerve.com

An ezine for online erotica. It is a "smart, honest magazine on sex, with cliché-shattering prose and fiction, as well as striking photographs of naked people that capture more than their flesh."

Planned Parenthood
www.plannedparenthood.org

Offers sexual health advice and family planning, counseling services, and education.

Salon
www.salon.com/sex

Called "intriguing and intelligent" by *The Washington Post* and "smart and provocative" by *Forbes* magazine, Salon is an ezine that takes an educated, intelligent look at sex, society, politics, and culture. The sex section features reviews and articles on sex in the film industry, new fiction, pornography, photography, online love, and more.

Sexual Health InfoCenter
www.sexhealth.org

A well-respected source for sexual health info, created in the "spirit that there should be open and honest discussion of human sexuality available." Channels include better sex, sex and aging, birth control, safe sex, sexual problems, sex tips, and a discussion forum.

Tabooboo
www.tabooboo.com

An online shopping site that sells products from all over the world, including vibrating and non-vibrating toys, bondage gear, condoms and oils, gifts and games, and fantasy wear. Products are delivered in a plain-covered box for privacy.

Women.com
www.women.com

In addition to the more standard women's-interest subjects, the site has a sex and dating area with articles on romance, relationships, better sex, solo sex, plus a boutique for shopping, sex tips and facts, a male anatomy quiz, a bisexual board, and more.

QUOTATION CREDITS

The publisher and author would like to thank the following sources for the quotations that appear throughout the book:

page 3: Sophia Loren, from *Halliwell's Filmgoer's Companion*, Flamingo, 1984.

page 14: Mae West, as Flower Belle Lee in the 1940 film *My Little Chickadee*.

page 25: Tallulah Bankhead, www.geocities.com/hollywood.

page 40: Mae West, from *Mae West on Sex*, Health and ESP, W. H. Allen, 1975.

page 55: Elton John, *Rolling Stone* magazine, October 1976.

pages 70 and 82: Marilyn Monroe, www.starspage.com.

page 97: Mae West, as Frisco Doll, in the 1936 film *Klondike Annie*.

other books by ulysses press

The Sexy Bitch's Book of Doing It, Getting It and Giving It
Flic Everett, $9.95

Dishes the dirty truth on everything from foreplay and oral sex to sex toys and fantasy games.

The Sexy Bitch's Book of Finding Him, Doing Him and Dating Him
Siobhan Kelly, $9.95

If you're ready to go out and get what you want, this book offers invaluable tips on everything from clothes and chat topics to the sexiest ways to undress and the most unforgettable things to do once you're naked.

The Little Bit Naughty Book of Sex
Dr. Jean Rogiere, $9.95

A handy pocket hardcover that is a fun, full-on guide to enjoying great sex.

The Wild Guide to Sex and Loving
Siobhan Kelly, $16.95

Packed with practical, frank and sometimes downright dirty tips on how to hone your bedroom skills, this handbook tells you everything you need to know to unlock the secrets of truly tantalizing sensual play.

To order these books call 800-377-2542 or 510-601-8301, fax 510-601-8307, e-mail ulysses@ulyssespress.com, or write to Ulysses Press, P.O. Box 3440, Berkeley, CA 94703. All retail orders are shipped free of charge. California residents must include sales tax. Allow two to three weeks for delivery.